Crisis Communication Planning and Strategies for Nonprofit Leaders

Crisis Communication Planning and Strategies for Nonprofit Leaders examines the unique position of nonprofit organizations in an intersection of providing public services and also being a part of Emergency and crisis management practices.

This text discusses the evolution of crisis communication planning, the unique position of nonprofit organizations and the crises they face, along with provision of conceptual and theoretical frameworks to generate effective crisis communication plans for nonprofit organizations to utilize within diverse crises. Through the use of innovative real-life case studies investigating the impact of crisis communication plans, this book provides the foundational knowledge of crisis communication planning, theoretically supported strategies, crisis typology and planning resources. Each chapter focuses on critical strategic planning concepts and includes a summary of key points, discussion questions and additional resources for each concept. With this text, nonprofit organizations will be able to strategically plan for organization-specific and emergency management related crises, develop effective crisis communication plans, garner internal and external support and generate assessment strategies to maintain the relevancy of these plans within their future endeavors.

Crisis Communication Planning and Strategies for Nonprofit Leaders offers a new and insightful approach to crisis communication planning to assist nonprofit organizations that are called upon to fulfill a variety of community needs, such as sheltering, food distribution, relief funding, family reunification services, volunteer mobilization and much more. It is an essential resource for nonprofit organizations.

Brittany "Brie" Haupt, Ph.D., is Assistant Professor at Virginia Commonwealth University in the Homeland Security & Emergency Preparedness Department, in Virginia, United States. Her research interests lie in cultural competency, emergency and crisis management, crisis communication and community resilience. She has published in *Public Administration Review, Journal of Public Affairs Education, Journal Nonprofit Management and Leadership, Journal of Homeland Security and Emergency Management, Disaster Prevention and Management, Risk, Hazards, and Crisis in Public Policy, Journal of Emergency Management* and *Frontiers in Communication* section "Disaster Communications". Dr. Haupt's award-winning book with Dr. Claire Connolly Knox, titled *Cultural Competence for Emergency and Crisis Management: Concepts, Theories, and Case Studies*, offers educators a roadmap for successfully engaging participants in various aspects of cultural competency knowledge, skills and abilities. This text received the American Society of Public Administration's Section on Democracy and Social Justice's 2021 Book of the Year Award.

Lauren Azevedo, Ph.D., is Assistant Professor at Penn State Harrisburg in the School of Public Affairs, in Pennsylvania, United States. Her experience as a grant writer with public and nonprofit organizations on program evaluation and capacity building and consulting with several of these agencies has helped shape her research agenda on nonprofit leadership. Her research focuses on nonprofit capacity building, nonprofit leadership and governance, and social equity. She has published in *Nonprofit Management and Leadership, Public Administration Review, Public Integrity* and the *Journal of Public Affairs Education*, among others. She has also presented her research at several national conferences including the American Evaluation Association (AEA), American Society for Public Administration (ASPA), the Network of Schools of Public Policy, Affairs, and Administration (NASPAA) and the Association for Research on Nonprofit Organizations and Voluntary Action (ARNOVA).

Crisis Communication Planning and Strategies for Nonprofit Leaders

Brittany "Brie" Haupt and
Lauren Azevedo

Routledge
Taylor & Francis Group

NEW YORK AND LONDON

First published 2023
by Routledge
605 Third Avenue, New York, NY 10158

and by Routledge
4 Park Square, Milton Park, Abingdon, Oxon, OX14 4RN

Routledge is an imprint of the Taylor & Francis Group, an informa business

ISBN: 978-0-367-70674-6 (hbk)
ISBN: 978-1-032-43539-8 (pbk)
ISBN: 978-1-003-14748-0 (ebk)

DOI: 10.4324/9781003147480

Typeset in Times New Roman
by Deanta Global Publishing Services, Chennai, India

This book is dedicated to my family and friends who supported me through this process. I also dedicate this book to nonprofit practitioners and academics who have faced difficult crises and persevered. Lastly, I give a special note to Dr. Lauren Azevedo, my friend and research colleague, who has supported me since my doctoral program and continues to have my back no matter what.

– Brittany "Brie" Haupt

To my family, for your endless support and patience, to my academic colleagues and friends, for your advice, wisdom and accountability, and to the nonprofits in our communities, whose work for the most vulnerable inspires me endlessly – this book is dedicated to you.

– Lauren Azevedo

Contents

Tables

Figures

Preface

Crisis Communication Planning and Strategies for Nonprofit Leaders examines the unique position of nonprofit organizations in the intersection of providing public services and also being a part of emergency and crisis management practices. Due to this complex positioning, nonprofits not only face the diverse hazards and disasters that emergency managers anticipate (i.e., natural disaster, civil/conflict and technological), but they also face organization-specific crises concerning their operation and reputation. This makes communication and public trust critical to their success. Unfortunately, one badly managed crisis can derail overarching strategic plans for their organization and any issue with their ability to operate or threats to their reputation can cause them to struggle for survival. It is imperative for nonprofit organizations to strategically plan for various types of crises the organization can face and develop crisis communication plans that support their mission, vision, values and the goals they want to achieve within the communities they serve. This text discusses the evolution of crisis communication planning, the unique position of nonprofit organizations and the crises they face, along with the provision of conceptual and theoretical frameworks to generate effective crisis communication plans for nonprofit organizations to utilize within diverse crises. Moreover, this text provides case studies to investigate the impact of crisis communication plans, or lack thereof, within real-life contexts.

The key aspect for nonprofit organizations is communication. Unfortunately, limited research has been conducted on crisis communication planning and its impact on the nonprofit sector and Nonprofit specific organizations; yet, it is evident that nonprofit organizations need to engage in crisis communication planning to mitigate the impact of crises they will face. Examples are abundant for nonprofits that have faced a crisis with detrimental results. Crises can lead to loss of donors, loss of political support and inability to meet the needs of their communities leaving their constituents to either stop receiving those services or search for another nonprofit to obtain the services. Moreover, their constituents are expecting communication that is considered open, honest, accurate, tailored, two-way and knowledgeable. More importantly, in the wake of the novel coronavirus pandemic (COVID-19), nonprofit organizations are realizing the need for crisis preparation and communication more than ever. There has been a renewed call for understanding how nonprofits can care for their employees and communities, as well as continue to serve their mission.

This text offers a new and insightful approach to crisis communication planning to assist nonprofit organizations that are called upon to fulfill a variety of community needs, such as sheltering, food distribution, relief funding, family reunification services, volunteer mobilization and much more. By providing the foundational knowledge of crisis communication planning, theoretically supported strategies, crisis typology and planning resources, this text is an essential resource for nonprofit organizations. Each chapter includes a focus on critical strategic planning concepts and a summary of key points and discussion questions. Moreover, this text incorporates innovative case studies and planning resources to aid any nonprofit leader. With this text, nonprofit organizations are able to strategically plan for organization-specific and emergency management-related crises, develop effective crisis communication plans, garner internal and external support and generate assessment strategies to maintain the relevancy of these plans within their future endeavors.

Chapter 1, "Nonprofit Organizations and Crises", examines the unique position of nonprofit organizations in the intersection of providing public services and being part of emergency management practices. Nonprofit organizations existing within this intersection not only face diverse hazards and disasters that emergency managers anticipate (i.e., natural disaster, civil/conflict and technological), but they also face organization-specific crises concerning their operation and reputation. Moreover, nonprofit organizations are called upon to fulfill a variety of community needs, such as sheltering, food distribution, relief funding, family reunification services, volunteer mobilization and much more. Understanding the critical role and responsibilities of nonprofit organizations is essential before moving forward to Chapter 2 on the evolution of crisis communication and management.

Chapter 2, "Crisis Communication and Management", focuses on the evolution of crisis communication and management along with its inclusion into the public and nonprofit sectors. Viewing management through the lens of a crisis approach incorporates the act of seeking to answer questions related to the immediate situation, understanding the unexpected event and finding opportunities within the chaos. Although the concept of crisis management began in the early 1980s, research regarding this arena did not start surfacing until later in the decade. The early research is characterized by its focus on organizational reputation and practitioners discussing how they managed issues and their personal experiences. This focus is consistent with the overarching goal of this text being instrumental to the success of nonprofit organizations when faced with diverse crises.

Chapter 3, "Crisis Communication Theories and Strategies", builds from Chapter 2 by discussing crisis communication theory and the research-based strategies formulated to the diverse crisis types facing the public and non-profit sectors. The main crisis communication theory for this text is situational crisis communication theory (SCCT). This theory broadens communication strategies found in general emergency management and crisis communication practice by providing a prescriptive system to connect response strategies to the crisis situation integrated with adaptations for local community needs and crisis typology. The emphasis on adaptation comes from the psychological nature of relating preparation, mitigation, response and recovery activities for crises to previous events and the automatic anticipation for future action. Therefore, SCCT becomes an essential approach for nonprofit organizations to adapt communication strategies based on the type of crisis and their knowledge of the local community's needs to assist their communities in more effectively preparing, mitigating, responding and recovering from crises. Moreover, integrating crisis communication strategies and knowledge of SCCT into a nonprofit manager's repertoire leads to enhancement of their knowledge, skills and abilities, as well as confidence in managing crises.

Chapter 4, "Governance Strategies and the Crisis Team", focuses on the governance of nonprofit organizations and how governance structure impacts crisis understanding and response. An overview of governance structure and board responsibilities is explored, focusing on risk management, communication and decision making. Several theories guide the foundation of board responsibility and risk assessment, including agency theory, stakeholder theory, resource dependency theory and managerial hegemony. These theories provide insight into how leaders understand, plan, lead and develop organizational policies that respond to crises. This chapter also explores crisis teams as leaders and their role in the governance structure. A sound governance structure is imperative to the nonprofit organization's mission, vision, values and the goals they want to achieve within the communities they serve.

Chapter 5, "Preparing for Crisis Communication Planning", examines what nonprofit organizations can do to prepare for strategically planning a crisis communication plan. This is a very intentional process, and the key to success is starting off on the right foot by establishing a planning agreement and conducting an initial assessment of the nonprofit organization to identify potential barriers and challenges to the process. The success of any crisis communication plan begins with this intentional preparation and sets the foundation for the remaining aspects of developing the plan, identifying and generating decision-making strategies and processes, communicating with internal and external stakeholders, implementing the plans and conducting evaluations and assessments.

Chapter 6, "The Crisis Communication Plan and Strategy Development", analyzes the components of an effective crisis communication plan and what attributes to incorporate in the strategic planning efforts. Moreover, this chapter focuses on the critical need to plan during non-crisis time periods as this allows for the time needed to brainstorm strategies, generate a crisis management organizational hierarchy, determine any resource or logistical needs, practice the plan with the organization's members as well as relevant community partners, collaborate with local emergency managers to check with the community's comprehensive emergency management plan and reduce duplication of efforts and identify any missing aspects, and to check with the nonprofit's legal team to determine any potential liabilities. All of these aspects assist with building the resilience capacity of the organization and have the best chance to reduce or eliminate any negative impact on the organization. This chapter also focuses on decision-making strategies and processes that drive the organization and the crisis communication plan both internally and externally.

Chapter 7, "Communication with Internal and External Stakeholders", highlights the pivotal role of internal and external stakeholders along with communication strategies to garner support. This is accomplished by understanding the organization's environment, as assessed in Chapter 6, and utilizing the information to engage in proactive conversations with internal and external stakeholders to support the goals and objectives of the crisis communication plans. Moreover, having these conversations during non-crisis periods allows for time to discuss any preconceived challenges and barriers along with providing an opportunity to practice the plan prior to activation.

Chapter 8, "Implementing the Crisis Communication Plan", speaks to implementing the crisis communication plan along with setting up a crisis communication center and discusses the importance of community connections. Utilizing practical experience of the author, the implementation process can be broken down into multiple phases: (1) the initiating phase to break down the strategic plan into logistical components where you identify how these strategies will be laid out in the organization; (2) the instructing phase to bring managers together and make sure they understand their role in this strategic implementation process and what feedback loops exist; (3) the adjusting phase where the organization engages in a trial period of sorts to see how it goes and to see what adjustments need to be made and then implement the crisis communication plan until an agreed-upon date where the evaluation and assessment process begins.

Chapter 9, "Evaluation and Assessment Strategies", presents evaluation and assessment strategies for crisis communication plans and ways to integrate the feedback into organizational policies and procedures. Focusing on the reassessment of strategies and the overall strategic planning process allows for ample time to prepare for a whole new round of strategic planning. It also allows organizations to come to the realization that planning never ends. If done intentionally, it is a continuous process. Reassessment of the crisis communication plans and strategies, along with the whole planning process, highlights how nonprofit organizations – the individuals and the entity as a whole – adapt to change and can continue operations despite challenges presented by a crisis.

Chapter 10, "Looking Back and Moving Forward: Adapting your Crisis Communication Plan", provides a summary of the previous chapters and provides insights for moving forward with crisis communication planning. Moreover, Chapter 10 speaks to nonprofit organization benchmarks, planning questions and considerations. Since this text has an audience of practitioners and educators, the authors will provide crisis communication planning tools to assist with the planning process and to justify necessary changes within the organization along with resources to help nonprofit organizations advocate for themselves and their communities.

Chapter 11 encompasses four case studies to provide space for examining and applying the concepts from chapters one through ten. Each case study provides an overview of a nonprofit organization impacted by a crisis along with discussion questions. The case studies include: (1) Give Kids The World and COVID-19; (2) Wounded Warrior Reputation; (3) People Inc. data breach; and (4) Association of Community Organizations for Reform Now scandal.

Additional tools are included in Appendix A in the format of a Crisis Communication Planning Worksheet.

1 Nonprofit Organizations and Crises

Lauren Azevedo

Nonprofit organizations are instruments for civil society that deliver public services and contribute to community development in many ways. Nonprofits serve communities in need in very specific ways when there is a lack of government or private resources or when necessary public programs are more efficiently or effectively delivered by community-based organizations. Researchers and economists have suggested that the sector emerged due to market failure, contract failure and high transaction costs, meaning the government is too slow, bureaucratic and lacking in ability to respond to local problems (Herman, 1994; Salaman, 1987; Weisbrod, 1975; 1978; Williamson, 1979).

Nonprofits stand at the forefront of providing social services to a demanding public and have proliferated to providing services formerly provided by all levels of government. Nonprofit organizations are separate and distinct from business and government agencies characterized as organized, self-governing entities, traditionally involving volunteerism and philanthropy, existing solely to serve the public, and mission driven (Herman, 1994; Salamon & Anheier, 1997). The nonprofit sector affords millions of people around the world an opportunity to come together to address important social issues. Private giving to local nonprofit social programs is one of the strengths of U.S. society (Herman, 1994; Salamon, 1999). Today the sector contributes over USD 985 billion to the U.S. economy (McKeever, 2018).

History of the U.S. Nonprofit Sector

Religious organizations performed most of the significant public services in the formative years of the United States. Education and welfare services were primarily coordinated by the churches. The history of U.S. philanthropy dates to the first colonial settlers. During this time, first nations demonstrated acts of kindness for survival by teaching colonists to grow

DOI: 10.4324/9781003147480-1

corn and fish. U.S. settlers established new governance systems and banded together to help one another to build houses, churches and schools, fight disease, share food and create transportation infrastructure (Philanthropy Trust, 2016). Churches played an important role by sponsoring programs and organizations to meet community needs – what might be considered a government responsibility today (Worth, 2016). U.S. nonprofits evolved out of this religious tradition of serving community needs (Chopko, 1992). The first nonprofit or "charitable" organizations in the "new world" were locally based hospitals and Harvard College, established in 1636. Later, Ben Franklin created the Free Library Company, the University of Pennsylvania and the Philadelphia Hospital. Although government funds were used to subsidize these efforts, all these organizations were separate and independent from the government (Grobman, 2005).

As the U.S. entered the Progressive Era, characterized by social activism and political reform, policies like labor laws and women's suffrage came to the forefront. This period also saw an increase in American wealth and ideals of empowerment and giving back. Andrew Carengie's Gospel of Wealth, released in 1889, likely contributed to the idea of donating to causes and promoted ideas of owing society. Many were drawn to the Young Men's Christian Association (YMCA), which had the first significant fundraising campaign in the U.S. This was the first time an organization hired a professional to oversee a campaign, set a time limit on raising funds, while also soliciting various sponsors. This set the tone for many current nonprofit governance and financial structures today.

The U.S. involvement in World War II also increased volunteer and fundraising activity. American citizens who were not involved in the war but had family and friends overseas came together to help with the war effort to send supplies overseas. The United Service Organization for National Defense (USO), established in 1941, became a leading organization to support military members and their families. USO was created because President Roosevelt wanted to unite several associations, including the Salvation Army, Young Men's and Young Women's Christian Associations and the National Catholic Community Services, among others, into one organization to help lift morale and offer support from home (USO, 2022).

The U.S. Civil Rights Movement was also a critical moment in the history of nonprofits, as we saw communities come together to organize and address more focused issues, such as food and clothing to Americans who lost their jobs during the movement and veterans returning home from Vietnam. In addition, the Internal Revenue Service (IRS) established the 501(c)(3) tax code, increasing government involvement in social and cultural welfare programs. A surge in applications for tax-exempt status created the "nonprofit sector" as we know it now, with a need for more guidelines, policies and research attention on the sector.

As we entered a new century, a boom in internet access and technology changed the sector significantly. Online giving, social media and instant access to information transformed the way nonprofits operate and connect with their constituents. Philanthropic giving steadily increased, and nonprofits began to see women and people of color holding staff and leadership positions. However, there are still significant strides to make in diversifying leadership and boardroom positions, particularly considering America's changing demographics and needs for equitable philanthropy (Azevedo et al., 2021). The novel coronavirus SARS-COV-2 COVID-19 pandemic and the social and political unrest in 2020 related to social justice, such as the Black Lives Matter (BLM) movement, taught us important lessons and are sending us into a new era of nonprofit management and leadership. Moving forward, the sector may refocus on the importance of partnerships and collaborations in building resilience, increase our understanding and relationships with diverse communities and better understand the multidimensional needs of vulnerable and marginalized populations, enhance advocacy efforts, strengthen lobbying for federal assistance during times of crisis, identify new and flexible strategies for communicating and programming, generate new financial structures and mechanisms and renew the focus on governance strategies, particularly for governance during times of crisis (McMullin & Raggo, 2020).

Growth of the Nonprofit Sector

The last few decades have seen tremendous growth within the U.S. nonprofit sector despite being situated in various political frameworks (Kim & Kim, 2015; McKeever & Pettijohn, 2014), which is echoed throughout the world. There are over 1.5 million U.S. nonprofits registered with the Internal Revenue Service (National Center for Charitable Statistics, 2019), a number that has increased over 10% since 2005 (McKeever, 2018). Globally, there are estimated to be over 10 million nongovernmental organizations (Nonprofit Action, 2015). This growth has placed a renewed emphasis on the importance of these organizations, including their societal contributions, role in government relations, accountability and financial structures, as well as the importance of philanthropy in disasters and the role of nonprofit organizations in crisis networks.

As the field of nonprofit management evolved, the role of nonprofit leaders developed significantly to better manage today and be responsive to diverse community needs. Lester Salamon (1999) identified that leaders have been responsive to shifts in financial structure and support, increased competition, impetus for effectiveness, and revolutions in technology.

These structural and organizational challenges are in addition to the social changes of the past few decades, including demographic shifts, innovative forms of philanthropy, increased visibility and policy salience, and renewed government spending, to name a few (Renz, 2016). Communities today are also facing deteriorating race relations, social stratification and economic division, which have led to a wellspring of many other social issues, such as equitable education, affordable housing, access to healthcare, unemployment and increased crime. With community needs as complex and multifaceted as ever, nonprofit leaders must equip themselves with necessary tools to be resilient.

Nonprofits as Vehicles for Community Response

The unique positioning of nonprofits within communities makes them well situated to respond to many of these complex social issues, mobilize volunteers and resources, build and develop community, increase activism, provide and tailor holistic services, innovate service delivery, promote social values, create civic activism and increase capacity and accessibility through co-production and community involvement (Almog-Bar, 2018; Bode & Brandsen, 2014), particularly in times of community unrest or uncertainty that surround crises. Nonprofit organizations have an important role in humanitarian relief and disaster response networks (Kapucu, 2006). They have more flexibility than government agencies in responding to crises (Steuerle, 2002) and can work collaboratively with other agencies to mobilize resources quickly.

Although nonprofits have historically mobilized citizens and resources during disasters, these efforts were not always organized. Initiatives and organizations utilizing collaborative capacity are the most effective for community crisis response. Organizations like the National Voluntary Organizations Active in Disaster (VOAD) were created to bring nonprofits together with government and private agencies to respond to disasters. Literature highlights the importance of collaborative capacity and the role of nonprofits in community response and resilience over the past two decades. This has certainly been the case in more recent crises, such as the terrorist attacks on September 11, 2001, Hurricane Katrina and the Boston Marathon Bombings. Within these crises, nonprofit organizations assisted in disaster response and recovery activities. They were called upon to work collaboratively with other agencies to fulfill a variety of needs, such as provide shelter, assist in food distribution, distribute relief funding, offer family reunification services, mobilize volunteers as well as many other responsibilities (Hu, Knox, & Kapucu, 2014; Kapucu, 2006; 2007; Kapucu, Yuldashev, & Feldheim 2011).

Nonprofit organizations also play a key role in lobbying and advocacy for victims in disasters, long-term policy development and the sector. The novel coronavirus SARS-COV-2 (COVID-19) pandemic highlights the most current case of many nonprofit organizations working on the forefront of the philanthropic response through advocacy and lobbying activities. In conjunction with the lobbying and advocacy efforts led by a coalition of nonprofits, there were critical provisions included by Congress in the CARES Act, which incorporated a demand for substantial assistance for nonprofits in the form of forgivable loans and operating grant support (Delaney, 2020). Efforts like these demonstrate the critical response, beyond service delivery and resource mobilization, that nonprofits are often taking on as localized experts on their communities.

Crises in Nonprofits

Although nonprofits are often on the forefront of community response to crises, they can also be directly involved in and impacted by a variety of crises. A *crisis* can be broadly defined as the perception and impact of an unpredictable event that may escalate, fall under stakeholder scrutiny, jeopardize reputation and stakeholder expectations or interfere with operations and can generate negative outcomes (Coombs, 2013; Fink, 1986). Within a complex and ever-changing environment, nonprofit leaders need to understand the types of crises they may face that threaten their resiliency and sustainability. A nonprofit crisis may include anything from a failed fundraising campaign, workplace violence or fake rumors, to a natural hazard, disease outbreak or terror situation, all of which are considered crises. Generally, we can divide nonprofit crises into either a *community crisis* or an *organizational crisis*, depending on whether the crisis is threatening the organization internally or externally and its relation to social constructs (involving people) or technical issues (involving procedures, systems, structures or society). Figure 1.1 shows the four broad ways to classify a nonprofit crisis. These categories include *organizational technical crisis*, *community technical crisis*, *organizational social crisis* and *community social crisis*, along with examples of crisis types within each category. Crises can range in intensity and severity and can be considered due to environmental threat or internal weaknesses (Egelhoff & Sen, 1992).

Although Figure 1.1 is adapted to nonprofit crises from corporate crisis situations, nonprofits have different considerations from businesses. Distinct differences for nonprofits from businesses, according to Frumkin (2002), include: not coercing participation, operating without profit distribution to shareholders and existing without clear lines of ownership. Nonprofits also exist for public benefit and are mission driven, which affords them tax-exempt status from the Internal Revenue Service (IRS). Citizens that donate

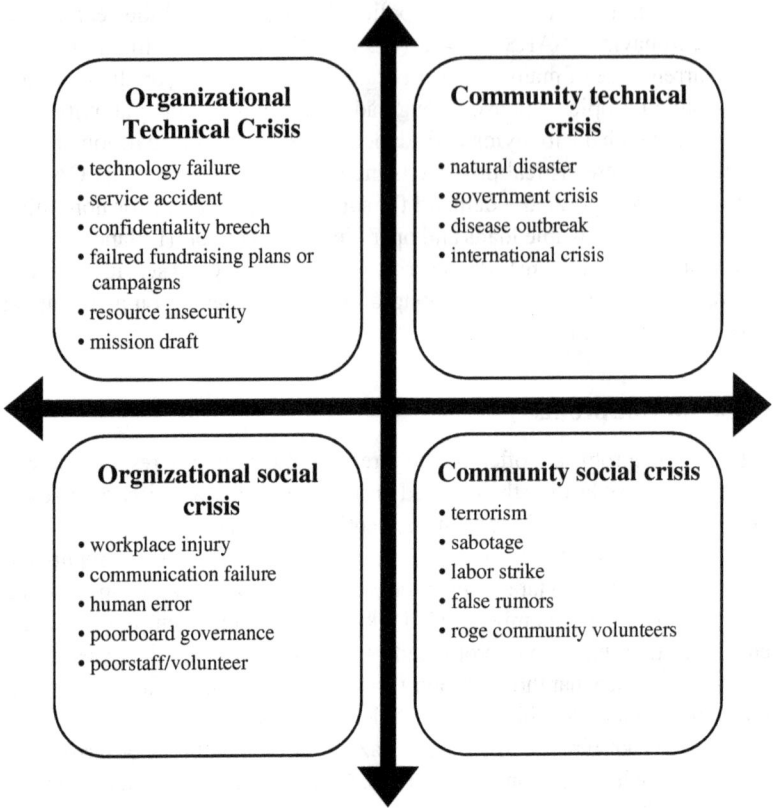

Figure 1.1 Types of Nonprofit Crises.

resources to nonprofits are placing faith in them that they will operate to fulfill their mission ethically and honestly. Thus, public trust is essential for nonprofit reputation.

Importance of Communication

Communication is a key aspect for nonprofits in handling crises. In its simplest form, communication is the transfer of information through some channel (verbal, email, body language, etc.) from one party to another. It is important to distinguish nonprofit communication from nonprofit *marketing* and nonprofit *storytelling*. Nonprofit marketing includes activities and messages that can motivate stakeholders to take action toward mission fulfillment and social change (Wymer, Knowles, & Gomes, 2006). *Storytelling* is sharing accounts or examples of the nonprofit's work and impact. Marketing and communications are both key parts of an organization's strategy, but marketing focuses on identifying stakeholders and communication is a tangible, tactical part of the marketing plan. Storytelling is a tool used in communication to help explain what an organization does and the type of impact it makes (Conrardy, 2019).

In *effective communication*, the receiver understands what the sender (messenger) intended (Denhardt et al., 2018). The communication process may be more complex when considering the goal of establishing shared meaning. This is because we often unintentionally misinterpret others' intent due to assumptions and bias. By understanding barriers to effective communication, we can aim to limit bias and produce more effective communication where included information is accurate, honest and produced in such a way the receiver understands, accepts and finds the information useful.

Barriers to effective communication are seen in Figure 1.2. These are needed as a poor choice of channels can cause misinterpretation of intent. These include:

- *perception*, or when the receiver processes information based on one's own experiences or viewpoints and misses original messenger intent;
- *semantics*, or when there are language differences between the sender and receiver that may include use of regional or unfamiliar expressions or difficulty understanding accents
- *organizational jargon*, or nonprofit terminology or acronyms that some individual receivers outside of the organization may not understand;
- *filtering*, or when the messenger distorts or withholds some information in an effort to manage the receiver's reactions;
- *overloading information*, or when the messenger overwhelms the receiver with details that distracts or confuse the receiver;
- *gender and/or cultural differences*, where social norms and gender differences can influence emotions expressed or interpreted; and finally
- *poor listening*, where the receiver's capacity to listen is insufficient regardless of the messenger's skill in communicating (Denhardt et al., 2018; Ikisesh, 2020; Lunenburg, 2010). Poor listening can happen for a number of reasons, including physical barriers (such as poor quality equipment or speakers, background noise or distance between communicators), psychological barriers (individuals dealing with anger or anxiety may struggle to listen effectively), structural barriers (inefficient communication systems within the nonprofit) or physiological barriers (deaf or hard of hearing, visual impairments, etc.).

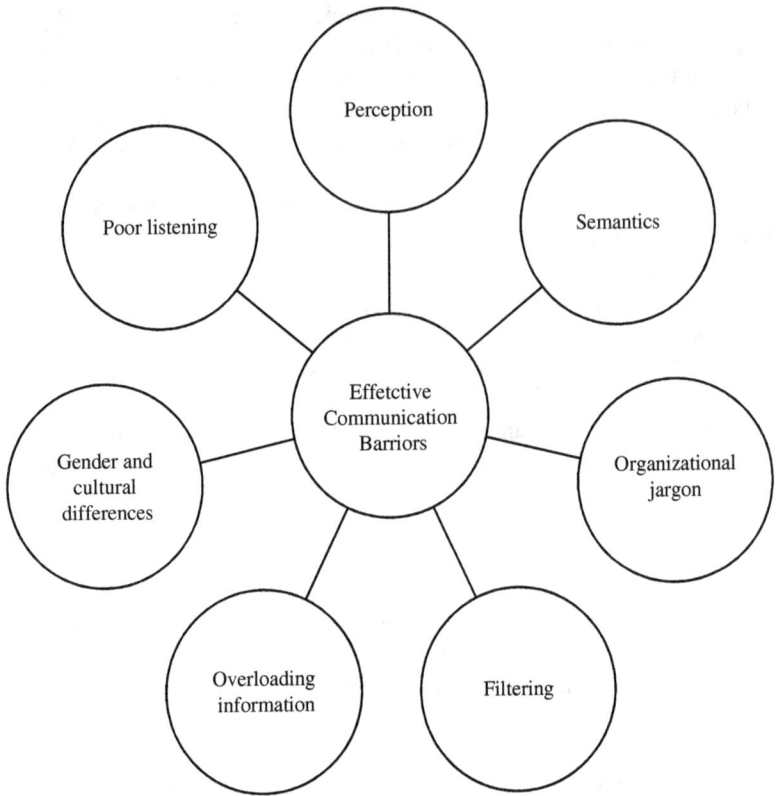

Figure 1.2 Barriers to Effective Communication.

Understanding these barriers improves the process of communication so non-profit communicators can be more effective. Developing awareness-related skill sets, such as patience and empathy, can also be helpful for improving communication quality. These barriers are important to remember when communicating during a crisis and planning for crisis communication.

Nonprofit Crisis Communication

Nonprofit crisis communication is important for upholding reputation and ultimately organizational success (Sisco, 2012). Nonprofit crisis communication is defined as gathering, processing and disseminating information on behalf of the nonprofit organization during a crisis. Reputation management is important because it can impact loyalty, financial success and attitudes toward the organization (Lyon & Cameron, 2004). How a nonprofit organization responds to a crisis can shape its perception well beyond the crisis. Thus, it is essential nonprofit leaders have well prepared their organization for crises of all types in their crisis communication plan.

The remaining chapters of this book examine the importance of communication during nonprofit crises, with a focus on nonprofit crisis communication plans that support the mission, vision, values and goals of the organization. A nonprofit *crisis communication plan* is a clear list of steps for a nonprofit organization to follow in case of an unexpected or before unprecedented event, including an organizational technical crisis, community technical crisis organizational social crisis or community social crisis. The plan includes how and when to communicate with stakeholders and how to prevent such crises from impacting the organization to the same extent in the future. In addition, each additional chapter will discuss the types of crises nonprofit organizations may face along with planning guidelines and theoretical frameworks. Chapter 2 will focus specifically on the evolution of crisis communication and management along with its inclusion into the public and nonprofit sectors.

Summary of Key Points

- The United States has a history of philanthropy and coming together to respond to community needs and crisis situations. Religious organizations fulfilled many public needs in early America.
- The nonprofit sector has seen tremendous growth in the past few decades, highlighting the need to focus on these organizations' societal contributions.
- Nonprofits are well positioned to contribute to their communities in many ways, including mobilizing resources and volunteers, increasing activism, providing holistic community services, innovating service delivery, promoting social values, building civic activism and community involvement and helping in disaster response.
- Nonprofit organizations have played key roles in disaster response and recovery networks, in roles such as providing shelter and food, mobilizing resources and volunteers and in advocacy and lobbying activities.
- Crises within nonprofits can be categorized by organization or community and by social or technical crises. These four categories include *organizational technical crisis, community technical crisis, organizational social crisis* and *community social crisis.*
- *Communication* is a key aspect for nonprofits in handling crises. We can ensure active, honest and meaningful information is communicated by identifying barriers to effective communication.

- A nonprofit *crisis communication plan* details the steps for a nonprofit to take during a crisis, including how and when to communicate with stakeholders.

Discussion Questions

1. How does the nonprofit sector differ from government and private sectors?
2. How have nonprofit leaders adapted to the tremendous growth of the nonprofit sector?
3. What is a nonprofit crisis and how can nonprofit crises be classified?
4. How has early American philanthropy evolved to shape community response to crisis?
5. Why is collaborative capacity important in nonprofit crisis response?
6. How can understanding barriers to communication assist nonprofit leaders during crisis?
7. Why is reputation management important in nonprofit organizations?

References

Almog-Bar, M. (2018, March). Civil society and nonprofits in the age of new public governance: Current trends and their implications for theory and practice. *Nonprofit Policy Forum, 8*(4), 343–349.

Azevedo, L., Gaynor, T. S., Shelby, K., & Santos, G. (2021). The complexity of diversity and importance for equitable philanthropy. *Nonprofit Management and Leadership, 31*(3), 595–607.

Bode, I., & Brandsen, T. (2014). State–third sector partnerships: A short overview of key issues in the debate. *Public Management Review, 16*(8), 1055–1066.

Chopko, M. E. (1992). Restoring Trust and Faith-Human Rights Abuses Do Happen, the Church Admits, but the Institution Has Not Closed Its Eyes. *Human Rights, 19*, 22.

Conrardy, A. (2019). *Marketing vs communications vs. storytelling*. Retrieved from https://prosper-strategies.com/nonprofit-storytelling-marketing -communications/.

Coombs, T. (2013). Situational theory of crisis: Situational crisis communication theory and corporate reputation. *The handbook of communication and corporate reputation*, 262–278.

Delaney, T. (2020). How nonprofits can utilize the new federal laws dealing with Covid-19. *Nonprofit Quarterly*. Retrieved from https://nonprofitquarterly.org/ how-nonprofits-can-utilize-the-new-federal-laws-dealing-with-covid-19/.

Denhardt, R. B., Denhardt, J. V., Aristigueta, M. P., & Rawlings, K. C. (2018). *Managing human behavior in public and nonprofit organizations*. Washington, DC: CQ Press.

Egelhoff, W. G., & Sen, F. (1992). An information-processing model of crisis management. *Management Communication Quarterly, 5*(4), 443–484.

Fink, S., & American Management Association. (1986). *Crisis management: Planning for the inevitable.* New York: Amacom.

Frumkin, P. (2002). *On Being Nonprofit.* Cambridge, Mass.: Harvard University Press.

Grobman, G. M. (2005). *The nonprofit handbook: Everything you need to know to start and run your nonprofit organization.* 4th edition. Charlottesville, VA: White Hat Communications.

Herman, R. (1994). *The handbook of nonprofit management and leadership.* San Francisco, CA: Jossey-Bass.

Hu, Q., Knox, C. C., & Kapucu, N. (2014). What have we learned since September 11, 2001? A network study of the Boston marathon bombings response. *Public Administration Review, 74*(6), 698–712.

Ikiseh, B. N. (2020). The internal communication barriers: A communication audit report of a nonprofit organisation. *Global Journal of Management And Business Research, 20*(6), 27–35.

Kapucu, N. (2006). Public nonprofit partnerships for collective action in dynamic contexts of emergencies. *Public Administration, 84*(1), 205–220.

Kapucu, N. (2007). Nonprofit response to catastrophic disasters. *Disaster Prevention and Management, 16*(4), 551–561.

Kapucu, N., Yuldashev, F., & Feldheim, M. A. (2011). Nonprofit organizations in disaster response and management: A network analysis. *European Journal of Economic and Political Studies, 4*(1), 83–112.

Kim, S. E., & Kim, Y. H. (2015). Measuring the growth of the nonprofit sector: A longitudinal analysis. *Public Administration Review, 75*(2), 242–251.

Lunenburg, F. C. (2010). Communication: The process, barriers, and improving effectiveness. *Schooling, 1*(1), 1–10.

Lyon, L., & Cameron, G. T. (2004). A relational approach examining the interplay of prior reputation and immediate response to a crisis. *Journal of Public Relations Research, 16*(3), 213–241.

McKeever, B. (2018). *The nonprofit sector in brief 2018.* The Urban Institute: National Center for Charitable Statistics. Retrieved from https://nccs.urban .org/publication/nonprofit-sector-brief-2018#the-nonprofit-sector-in-brief-2018 -public-charites-giving-and-volunteering.

McKeever, B., & Pettijohn, S. L. (2014). *The nonprofit sector in brief.* The Urban Institute: National Center for Charitable Statistics. Retrieved from https:// community-wealth.org/sites/clone.community-wealth.org/files/downloads/ report-mckeever-pettijohn.pdf.

McMullin, C., & Raggo, P. (2020). Leadership and governance in times of crisis: A balancing act for nonprofit boards. *Nonprofit and Voluntary Sector Quarterly, 49*(6), 1182–1190.

Mitroff, I. I., Pauchant, T. C., & Shrivastava, P. (1988). The structure of man-made organizational crises: Conceptual and empirical issues in the development of a general theory of crisis management. *Technological Forecasting and Social Change, 33*(2), 83–107.

National Center for Charitable Statistics. (2019). *The nonprofit sector in brief.* Retrieved from https://nccs.urban.org/project/nonprofit-sector-brief.

Nonprofit Action. (2015). *Facts and stats about NGOs worldwide.* Retrieved from http://nonprofitaction.org/2015/09/facts-and-stats-about-ngos-worldwide/.

Philanthropic Trust. (2016). *A history of modern philanthropy.* Retrieved from https://www.historyofgiving.org/introduction/.

Renz, D. O. (2016). *The Jossey-Bass handbook of nonprofit leadership and management.* Hoboken, NJ: John Wiley & Sons.

Salaman, L. M. (1987). *Partners in public service; The scope and theory of government nonprofit relations.* In The Nonprofit Sector: A Research Handbook, 99-1 IT.Ed.

Salamon, L. M. (1999). The nonprofit sector at a crossroads: The case of America. *VOLUNTAS: International Journal of Voluntary and Nonprofit Organizations, 10*(1), 5–23.

Salamon, L. M., & Anheier, H. K. (Eds.). (1997). *Defining the nonprofit sector: A cross-national analysis.* New York: Manchester University Press.

Sisco, H. F. (2012). Nonprofit in crisis: An examination of the applicability of situational crisis communication theory. *Journal of Public Relations Research, 24*(1), 1–17.

Steuerle, E. (2002). *Managing charitable giving in the wake of disaster.* The Urban Institute: National Center for Charitable Statistics. Retrieved from https://www.urban.org/sites/default/files/publication/60056/310471-Managing-Charitable-Giving-in-the-Wake-of-Disaster.PDF.

United Service Organizations. (2022). *The organization: Our mission.* Retrieved from https://www.uso.org/about.

Weisbrod, B. A. (1975). Toward a theory of the voluntary non-profit sector in a three sector economy. In E. S. Phelps (Ed.), *Altruism, morality, and economic theory* (pp. 171–196). New York: Russell Sage Foundation.

Weisbrod, B. A. (1978). *The voluntary nonprofit sector.* Lexington, KY: Lexington Books.

Williamson, O. E. (1979). Transaction-cost economies: The governance of contractual relations. *Journal of Law and Economics, 22*(2), 233–61.

Worth, M. J. (2016). *Fundraising: Principles and practice.* Thousand Oaks, CA: Sage Publications, Inc.

Wymer, W., Knowles, P., & Gomes, R. (2006). *Nonprofit marketing: Marketing management for charitable and nongovernmental organizations.* Thousand Oaks, CA: Sage Publications, Inc.

2 Crisis Communication and Management

Brittany "Brie" Haupt and Lauren Azevedo

Evolution of Crisis Communication and Management

Determining the start of crisis communication and crisis management as a field is difficult to ascertain, although many attribute its beginning to the 1980s tampering incident within the Johnson & Johnson organization regarding its Tylenol product. The product tampering case led to the death of seven individuals from Chicago due to poison within the product, and the backlash had a significant impact on consumers and businesses at that time (Coombs, 2014). The interest grew exponentially in crisis management, specifically for corporate organizations, as society and businesses began to realize how negative consequences of improper management could have a resounding impact on their bottom line and resilience.

> Crisis management as a profession took form and became a field where individuals sought to mitigate or diminish the negative impact of a crisis and protect organizational image from stakeholder perception (Coombs, 2014).

In terms of a definition, crisis management is "a set of factors designed to combat crises and to lessen the actual damage inflicted" (p. 5). The process of lessening the impact spans across time-specific phases of pre-crisis, crisis and post-crisis. *Pre-crisis period* is the state of an organization prior to a crisis occurring. The *crisis period* is when a crisis has impacted the organization and the ripple effect of the impact is discernible. The *post-crisis period* occurs when the crisis has reached some level of resolution and operations of the organization are resumed. The operational definition provided by Sellnow and Seeger (2013) states,

> crisis communication could simply be understood as the ongoing process of creating shared meaning among and between groups,

DOI: 10.4324/9781003147480-2

communities, individuals and agencies, within the ecological context of a crisis, for the purpose of preparing for and reducing, limiting and responding to threats and harm (p. 13).

Although the concept of crisis management began in the early 1980s, research in this arena did not start surfacing until later in the decade (Coombs, 2014). The early research is characterized by its focus on organizational reputation and practitioners discussing how they managed issues and their personal experiences. With the Tylenol case being considered a catalyst for this field, the critical importance was cemented with the Challenger explosion in 1986. These two events led to research focusing on decision-making and emphasizing *rhetorical analysis*. It created what is known as *Apologia*, which became a dominant theory with researchers focusing on what managers said and did to address crises and their lack of acknowledgment for impacted stakeholders (Coombs, 2014; Dionisopoulos & Vibbert, 1988).

Within the 1990s, crisis communication exploded due to research driven by the field of public relations. Publications and case studies came about focusing on corporate apologia, *image restoration theory* and situational crisis communication theory (SCCT) (Benoit, 1995; Coombs, 2012; Hearit, 1994; Ice, 1991). The theoretical surge was supported by evidence-based research and management implications. Entering into the 2000s, interest in crisis communication increased within fields related to communication, but the management arena keeps its stronghold along with organizational psychology (Coombs, 2012).

The expansion of crisis communication resulted in national and international conferences, new theories (i.e., contingency theory) and practical models for implementation (i.e., integrated crisis mapping) (Cameron, Pang, & Jin, 2007; Jin & Pang, 2010). Continued research in the area also created a distinction surrounding macro (large-scale) versus micro (small-scale) conceptualizations of crisis communication. Research also focused on how macro or micro crises influenced practice and implementation of crisis communication plans along with identifying stages of communication (Drupsteen & Guldenmund, 2014) (i.e., pre-crisis, during and post-crisis) and the cycle of communication (Norris et al., 2008) (i.e., adjusting, sharing and instructing) (Coombs & Holladay, 2002; Frandsen & Johansen, 2010; Ulmer, Seeger, & Sellnow, 2017).

Research on the stages of information found there were distinct differences between how organizations would communicate before a crisis, during a crisis and after a crisis. These differences impacted how stakeholders viewed the response to a crisis and the overall reputation of the organization.

The cycle of communication incorporates adjusting, sharing and instructing phases. The *adjusting phase* is how organizations adjust their crisis communication plan to the type of crisis they are facing. *Sharing* focuses on how the organization shares information on their crisis communication plan along with any adaptations. *Instructing* is how the organization prepares and supports entities that are involved in the implementation of the crisis communication plan. The introduction of social media continued the expansion of crisis communication and available strategies with a new focus on marketing. In essence, crisis communication has gone global.

Communication as an Intentional Activity

The perspective of communication is seen as an intentional activity, as it incorporates the intention of communication and is connected to the areas of transmission and information processing, crisis communication and risk communication (Anderson, 2016). It is important to note crisis communication differs from the field of risk communication (Reynolds & Seeger, 2005; Walker, 2012). Whereas risk communication is focused more on threats to public health and methods to reduce harm, crisis communication is focused more on a specific event, what is known and not known, the scope of impact and is principally informative. *Risk communication* focuses on the expressions' influence on behavior whereas crisis communication places importance on rhetoric (Anderson, 2016; Griffin et al., 2010; Reynolds & Seeger, 2005). Essentially, risk communication is "a process of sharing information about hazards, risks, vulnerability, assets, and adaptive mechanisms within organizations or with the public. The process is intentional and goal directed" (Pine, 2015, p. 186). Additionally, risk communication arguably addresses cultural and social factors more so than crisis communication due to its implementation in arenas like public health where the messages are being interpreted by a culturally diverse audience (Reynolds & Seeger, 2005). The ability of nonprofit and crisis management practitioners to understand all the needs of their community and generate a stable system for delivering critical information is time-intensive and complex (Paton & Johnston, 2001) with the most important aspects of communication consisting of the sources, channels, and messages (Lindell & Perry, 2007; Walker, 2012). *Sources* are characterized by their expertise and trustworthiness. *Channels* are organized by type and number (i.e., radio, brochures, face-to-face, etc.). *Messages* consist of the information provided about hazards, and the protective measures are characterized via comprehensibility, specificity and number. Practitioners and researchers soon began to notice disconnects between the sources of information, communication channels or communication tools utilized, and messages being released. Issues arose concerning:

- the anticipation of community needs;
- adaptation of communication for crisis type;
- information release before, during and after a crisis;
- lack of initiative to communicate;
- inadequate or incompatible communication technology;
- variations in values and norms;
- high levels of stress and pressure on individuals and teams;
- rapid event shifts and changing information;
- tension with media and the public;
- poor information-gathering capacities;
- inability to convey accurate information and its meaning; and
- cognition and collaboration (Benson, 1988; Bharosa, Lee, & Janssen, 2010; Chandler, 2010; Coombs, 2012; Walker, 2012).

Although the intent of these communication streams was well-intentioned, the impact varied due to how the message was sent, received, applied and reacted to (Benson, 1988; Phillips & Morrow, 2007).

Every communication situation during a crisis must be approached with consideration of many dynamics. Therefore, communicated messages are complex and ambiguous at the same time. Successful public communication seeks to balance the needs and expectations of diverse audiences and speak to each of them while not miscommunicating to the remainder (Chandler, 2010). Without an explicit design, the communication processes utilized may consist of serious constraints due to uncertainty of risk and the when, where, what, how and why (Comfort & Haase, 2006; Coombs, 2012).

The complexity of communication makes the need for planning quintessential.

Crisis Management and Inclusion in Planning Efforts

Where a disaster was viewed, and potentially defined, as an event that is seen collectively as a harmful episode, a crisis is considered when "a community of people – an organization, a town or a nation – perceives an urgent threat to core values or life-sustaining functions, which must be dealt with under conditions of uncertainty" (Boin & McConnell, 2007, p. 42). In terms of its origin, Boin and McConnell (2007) discussed the Greek and Chinese connections to the term *crisis* and highlighted references to a critical point, a fork in the road, a threat, an opportunity and a critical phase. Moreover, the term *crisis* has been applied to a diverse range of situations from natural hazards and environmental threats to infrastructural dramas, financial meltdowns or organizational decline. More recently, Coombs (2012) generated crisis types to include natural hazards, workplace violence, rumors, malevolence, challenges, technical-error accidents, technical-error product harm, human-error accidents, human-error product harm and organization misdeeds. According to Boin and McConnell (2007), "What all these dramatic events have in common is that they create impossible conditions for those who seek to manage the response operation and have to make urgent decisions while essential information about causes and consequences remains unavailable" (p. 43).

> Viewing management through the lens of a crisis approach incorporates the act of seeking to answer questions related to the immediate situation, understanding the unexpected event, and finding opportunities within the chaos (Boin & McConnell, 2007; Rosenthal, Boin, & Comfort, 2001; Toft & Reynolds, 2016).

As defined in Chapter 1, a *crisis* can be broadly defined as the perception and impact of an unpredictable event that may escalate, fall under stakeholder scrutiny, jeopardize reputation and stakeholder expectations, or interfere with operations and can generate negative outcomes (Coombs, 2012; Fink, 1986). In terms of the current National Incident Management System (NIMS), developed by the Federal Emergency Management Agency (2015a),

> a traditional, all-hazards approach to assisting communities during the life cycle of a disaster (i.e., preparation, mitigation, response, and recovery) influences the adjustment of emergency management information and communication.

Preparation involves increasing the readiness for potential disasters or hazards. Mitigation focuses on prevention and reduction of potential impact through (a) changing the nature of the threat, (b) decreasing vulnerability and (c) reducing exposure. The response component incorporates the community's capacity to monitor, predict, avoid, and reduce potential damage or address potential threats along with strengthening preparation activities for responding to disasters and assisting those impacted (Kapucu, Hawkins, & Rivera, 2013; Norris et al., 2008; Kapucu & Özerdem, 2011; McEntire, 2007; Sylves, 2014; Waugh & Streib, 2006; Toft & Reynolds, 2016).

Since it cannot be fully predicted how a crisis will affect local communities, trust and reliance are placed within an incident command system (ICS). This centralized command and control structure incorporates five dimensions (i.e., command, operations, planning, logistics, and finance and administration) and may include a public information officer, safety officer and a liaison (Boin & O'Connell, 2007; FEMA, 2015b). The main benefit of ICS is the ability for unified command and collaboration between local, state and federal stakeholders (Hu, Knox, & Kapucu, 2014); however, major challenges include lack of flexibility and adaptive capability of the system, growing complexity of communication needs for citizens and variations in the organizational hierarchy on local levels (Birkland, 2009; Hu, Knox, & Kapucu, 2014; Liu, Guo, & Nault, 2014).

In order to address these challenges, FEMA (2011) developed a whole-community perspective to emergency management practice and expanded the significance of crisis-related activities.

> Broadening responsibility from a government-centric to a community engagement perspective, FEMA (2011) promoted a deeper understanding of community complexity, recognition of capabilities and needs, intentional relationships with leaders, support of critical partnerships, empowerment of local action and leverage of infrastructure, networks and assets.

As stated by FEMA Administrator Craig Fugate (2015):

> We need to move away from the mindset that the Federal and State governments are always in the lead, and build upon the strengths of our local communities and, more importantly, our citizens. We must treat individuals and communities as key assets rather than liabilities.

Through their efforts, a plan was generated focusing on national emergency communication and providing guidance to practitioners and administrators. The *National Emergency Communications Plan* (NECP) specifically addresses: governance and leadership to enhance coordination, planning and decision-making; planning and procedures in terms of assessing and improving emergency management communications and their readiness for dynamic environments; improving capabilities for responders to communicate and coordinate through exercise and training programs; operational coordination to improve the effectiveness of operations through the communication of, and for, resources, personnel and capabilities across the community; and research and development to evaluate and support responders and unveil innovative capabilities (DHS, 2014).

The NECP was established to help local, state and tribal emergency management practitioners strategically plan and incorporate seven objectives (DHS, 2014). The first is the creation of formal decision-making structures and designation of leaders to coordinate emergency communications capabilities. Second is the promotion of federal programs and initiatives to enhance collaboration and align with national goals. The third is the employment of common planning and operational protocols to intentionally utilize personnel and resources. The fourth relates to emerging technologies to be integrated into current communication structures and be available for research, development, testing and evaluation. Fifth, in terms of responders, there must be a shared vision and approach to training and exercises to improve expertise and enhance response capabilities. Sixth focuses on the advancement of emergency communication within and between all levels, strategic planning efforts must integrate public–private partnerships and develop procedures as well as allocate resources. Lastly, preparation, mitigation, response and recovery capabilities must be implemented during all significant events.

Overall, the NECP provides a guiding tool for decision-makers and policymakers to examine their emergency management, or crisis, communication in a way to develop more effective policies and procedures (DHS, 2014). The emphasis on assessment connects to the need for understanding local community needs and identifying areas of vulnerability where the community's resilience capacity could be affected. Intentional assessment and strategic planning related to overcoming any potential areas that may negatively affect resilience leads to information necessary for emergency managers. This information may lead to more insightful or detailed plans, action-related messages for community members, new stakeholders or partners that will aid in related activities and tasks, or policies that do not currently exist.

Although there are general guidelines and frameworks to assist public entities in crisis communication efforts, there are limited resources for nonprofit organizations. Within this text, strategies for nonprofit organizations will be discussed and a planning framework is incorporated. Even though more detail will be provided in subsequent sections, there are general best practices for crisis communication efforts.

> To support effective crisis communication, nonprofit managers should operate in such a way that information collection, organization and dissemination leads to messages characterized as open, honest, accurate, tailored, two-way and knowledgeable (Haupt & Azevedo, 2021).

Other identified best practices include:

- promoting effective communication regarding process approaches and policy development;
- pre-event planning;
- partnerships with the public;
- listening to the public's concerns and understanding the audience;
- collaboration and coordination with credible sources;
- meeting the needs of the media and remaining accessible;

- communicating with empathy and concern;
- accepting uncertainty and ambiguity; and
- promoting self-efficacy (Seeger, 2006).

The more attention that a [nonprofit manager] can give to providing information on hazards, risk, and protective measures in non-crisis situations, the more likely it is that such information communicated during an actual emergency will result in adaptive citizen actions.

(Perry & Nigg, 1985, p. 76)

Essentially, the more the attention given to crisis communication strategies, the more resilient an organization can become.

Summary of Key Points

- The perspective of communication is seen as an intentional activity.
- A *crisis* can be broadly defined as the perception and impact of an unpredictable event that may escalate, fall under stakeholder scrutiny, jeopardize reputation and stakeholder expectations, or interfere with operations and can generate negative outcomes (Coombs, 2012; Fink, 1986).
- Crisis management took form and became a field where individuals sought to mitigate or diminish the negative impact of a crisis and protect stakeholders.
- The inability of nonprofit and emergency management practitioners to understand all the needs of their community and generate a stable system for delivering critical information is time-intensive and complex.
- To support effective crisis communication, nonprofit managers should operate in such a way that information collection, organization and dissemination lead to messages characterized as open, honest, accurate, tailored, two-way and knowledgeable.

Discussion Questions

1. How does viewing communication through the lens of a crisis impact decisions?
2. What aspects are there when considering crisis communication?
3. How does crisis communication connect to management?
4. How can nonprofit organizations support effective crisis communication?

References

Andersen, N. B. (2016). Analysing communication processes in the disaster cycle. In Dahlberg, R., O. Rubin, & M. T. Vendelo (Eds.), *Disaster research: Multidisciplinary and international perspectives*. Routledge Humanitarian Studies Series. London.

Benoit, W. L. (1995). *Accounts, excuses, and apologies: A theory of image restoration strategies*. SUNY Press: New York, NY.

Benson, J. A. (1988). Crisis revisited: An analysis of strategies used by Tylenol in the second tampering episode. *Communication Studies, 39*(1), 49–66.

Bharosa, N., Lee, J., & Janssen, M. (2010). Challenges and obstacles in sharing and coordinating information during multi-agency disaster response: Propositions from field exercises. *Information Systems Frontiers, 12*(1), 49–65.

Birkland, T. A. (2009). Disasters, lessons learned, and fantasy documents. *Journal of Contingencies and Crisis Management, 17*(3), 146–156.

Boin, A., & McConnell, A. (2007). Preparing for critical infrastructure breakdowns: The limits of crisis management and the need for resilience. *Journal of Contingencies and Crisis Management, 15*(1), 50–59.

Cameron, G. T., Pang, A., & Jin, Y. (2007). Contingency theory: Strategic management of conflict in public relations. In *Public relations: From theory to practice* (pp. 134–157). Research Collection Lee Kong Chian School Of Business. Singapore.

Chandler, R. C. (2010). *Emergency notification*. ABC-CLIO, Santa Barbara, CA.

Comfort, L. K., & Haase, T. W. (2006). Communication, coherence, and collective action the impact of Hurricane Katrina on communications infrastructure. *Public Works Management & Policy, 10*(4), 328–343.

Coombs, W. T. (2012). *Ongoing crisis communication: Planning, managing, and responding*. Sage Publications: Thousand Oaks, CA.

Coombs, W. T. (2014). State of crisis communication: Evidence and the bleeding edge. *Research Journal of the Institute for Public Relations, 1*(1), 1–12.

Coombs, W. T., & Holladay, S. J. (2002). Helping crisis managers protect reputational assets initial tests of the situational crisis communication theory. *Management Communication Quarterly, 16*(2), 165–186.

Department of Homeland Security. (2014). *National emergency communications plan*. Retrieved from http://www.dhs.gov/sites/default/files/publications/2014%20National%20Emergency%20Communications%20Plan_October%2029%202014.pdf.

Dionisopoulos, G. N., & Vibbert, S. L. (1988). CBS vs. Mobil Oil: Charges of creative bookkeeping in 1979. In H. R. Ryan (Ed.), *Oratorical encounters* (pp. 241–251). Greenwood: New York, NY.

Drupsteen, L., & Guldenmund, F. W. (2014). What is learning? A review of the safety literature to define learning from incidents, accidents and disasters. *Journal of Contingencies and Crisis Management, 22*(2), 81–96.

Federal Communications Commission. (2014). *Emergency communications guide*. Retrieved from http://www.fcc.gov/public-safety.

22 *Crisis Communication and Management*

Federal Emergency Management Agency. (2011). *A whole community approach to emergency management: Principles, themes, and pathways for action.* Retrieved from http://www.fema.gov/media-library-data/20130726-1813-25045-0649/whole_community_dec2011__2_.pdf.

Federal Emergency Management Agency. (2015a). *National preparedness system.* Retrieved from https://www.fema.gov/national-preparedness.

Federal Emergency Management Agency. (2015b). *National incident command system.* Retrieved from https://www.fema.gov/incident-command-system-resources.

Fink, S. (1986). Crisis management: Planning for the inevitable. Amacom.

Frandsen, F., & Johansen, W. (2010). Crisis communication, complexity, and the cartoon affair: A case study. In Timothy Coombs and Sharry Holliday (Eds.), *The handbook of crisis communication* (pp. 425–448). Blackwell Publishing: Oxford, England.

Griffin, E. A., Crossman, J., Bordia, S., Mills, C., Maras, S., Pearse, G., ... & Shanahan, D. (2010). *A first look at communication theory.* Boston: McGraw-Hill Higher Education, 230–265.

Haupt, B., & Azevedo, L. (2021). Crisis communication planning and nonprofit organizations. *Disaster Prevention and Management: An International Journal, 30*(2), 163–178.

Hearit, K. M. (1994). Apologies and public relations crises at Chrysler, Toshiba, and Volvo. *Public Relations Review, 20*(2), 113–125.

Hu, Q., Knox, C. C., & Kapucu, N. (2014). What have we learned since September 11, 2001? A network study of the Boston marathon bombings response. *Public Administration Review, 74*(6), 698–712.

Ice, R. (1991). Corporate publics and rhetorical strategies: The case of Union Carbide's Bhopal crisis. *Management Communication Quarterly, 4*(3), 341–362.

Jin, Y., & Pang, A. (2010). Future directions of crisis communication research: Emotions in crisis–The next frontier. In Timothy, Coombs & Sharry Holliday (Eds.), *Handbook of crisis communication* (pp. 677–682). Blackwell Publishing: Oxford, England.

Kapucu, N., Hawkins, C. V., & Rivera, F. I. (Eds.). (2013). *Disaster resiliency: Interdisciplinary perspectives.* Routledge: Oxfordshire, United Kingdom.

Kapucu, N., & Özerdem, A. (2011). *Managing emergencies and crises.* Jones & Bartlett Publishers.

Lindell, M. K., & Perry, R. W. (2007). Planning and preparedness. In Waugh, W. L. Jr. & K. Tierney (Eds.), *Emergency management: Principles and practice for local governments* (pp. 113–139). International City/County Management Association.

Liu, Y., Guo, H., & Nault, B. R. (2014). *Centralized versus decentralized provision of public safety networks.* Technology, 1–47.

McEntire, D. A. (2007). *Disaster response and recovery: Strategies and tactics for resilience.* New Jersey: Wiley.

Norris, F. H., Stevens, S. P., Pfefferbaum, B., Wyche, K. F., & Pfefferbaum, R. L. (2008). Community resilience as a metaphor, theory, set of capacities, and strategy for disaster readiness. *American Journal of Community Psychology, 41*(1–2), 127–150.

Paton, D., & Johnston, D. (2001). Disasters and communities: Vulnerability, resilience and preparedness. *Disaster Prevention and Management: An International Journal, 10*(4), 270–277.

Perry, R. W., & Nigg, J. M. (1985). Emergency management strategies for communicating hazard information. *Public Administration Review, 45*, 72–77.

Pine, J. (2015). *Hazards analysis: Reducing the impact of disasters.* CRC Press: Boca Raton, FL.

Phillips, B. D., & Morrow, B. H. (2007). Social science research needs: Focus on vulnerable populations, forecasting, and warnings. *Natural Hazards Review, 8*(3), 61–68.

Reynolds, B., & Seeger, M. W. (2005). Crisis and emergency risk communication as an integrative model. *Journal of Health Communication, 10*(1), 43–55.

Rosenthal, U., Boin, A., & Comfort, L. K. (2001). *Managing crises: Threats, dilemmas, opportunities.* Charles C Thomas Publisher: Boca Raton, FL.

Seeger, M. W. (2006). Best practices in crisis communication: An expert panel process. *Journal of Applied Communication Research, 34*(3), 232–244.

Sellnow, T. L., & Seeger, M. W. (2013). *Theorizing crisis communication (Vol. 4).* John Wiley & Sons: Hoboken, NJ.

Sylves, R. (2014). *Disaster policy and politics: Emergency management and homeland security.* CQ Press: Washington, D.C.

Toft, B., & Reynolds, S. (2016). *Learning from disasters.* Springer: New York, NY.

Ulmer, R. R., Sellnow, T. L., & Seeger, M. W. (2017). *Effective crisis communication: Moving from crisis to opportunity.* Sage Publications: Thousand Oaks, CA.

Walker, D. C. (2012). *Mass notification and crisis communications: Planning, preparedness, and systems.* CRC Press: Boca Raton, FL.

Waugh, W. L., & Streib, G. (2006). Collaboration and leadership for effective emergency management. *Public Administration Review, 66*(s1), 131–140.

3 Crisis Communication Theories and Strategies

Brittany "Brie" Haupt

Introduction

In terms of basic crisis communication strategies, a timeline approach is promoted where communication occurs before, during and after the crisis. Within these stages, there is a distinction between managing information and managing meaning (Coombs, 2012). Within the pre-crisis, or before, stage, it is critical for responsible officials to focus on planning and preparation. The more effective leader is one who is knowledgeable about policies and procedures and goes through training and exercises to determine any potential challenges. The crisis response, or during, stage focuses more on the implementation of policies and procedures and differentiating how a leader will react to the crisis and adapt communication strategies. The post-crisis, or after, stage concerns follow-up with stakeholders and returning to a sense of calm before preparing for the next event.

Speaking to emergency management and crisis communication strategies, research has discussed the impact of communication before, during and after a disaster or hazard with an emphasis on information collection, organization and dissemination (Chandler, 2010; Kapucu, Hawkins, & Rivera, 2013; Kapucu & Özerdem, 2011; McEntire, 2007; Sylves, 2014; Waugh & Streib, 2006), as well as strategies to aid in generating timely and comprehensible messages that meet the diverse needs of its audiences (Ulmer, Sellnow, & Seeger, 2017; Walker, 2012).

> The general recommendations and considerations revolve around: (1) how to transfer the message; (2) when to send the message; (3) will the recipient see, read or hear the message; (4) is the message comprehensible; and (5) what will be the response.

Boin and McConnell (2007) discussed the diversity of perspectives connected to the range of social sciences. Within the discipline of sociology,

DOI: 10.4324/9781003147480-3

the disaster perspective views a crisis as a phase in which institutions stop functioning. These phases are time-limited, and the functioning, or performance, of an institution or organization is impacted to the point of stopping all actions until the event ends. Additionally, sociologists incorporated a silver lining thought stream as a crisis was viewed as an opportunity for growth and change. Although crisis research was not deemed a niche within sociological research, the subfield of organization theory was integrated within a disaster event and formulated one of the most powerful theories for the crisis approach (Boin & McConnell, 2007). The inquiry into organizational theory then created a bridge between sociology and psychology and connects to the work done regarding safety research and decision-making (Diesing, 1992; Flin, 1996; Klein, 1999; Reason, 1990). The decision-making research led to international crises as well as political science. Entering into these arenas led to a focus on leadership, conflicts and subjectivity (Allison, 1971; Boin & McConnell, 2007; George, 1991; Hermann, 1972; Herek, Janis, & Huth, 1987; Lebow, 1984).

Within the political science arena, crises were studied more with the lens of structure and function (Almond, Flanagan, & Mundt, 1973; Boin & McConnell, 2007; Keeler, 1993; Rosenthal, Boin, & Comfort, 2001; Smith & Larimer, 2016; Stern, 1997). In some research, the crisis was a necessary component that led toward a more democratic society (Almond, Flanagan, & Mundt, 1973; Boin & McConnell, 2007). Shifting toward the advancement of business management, research began to incorporate a focus on reputation damage and business continuity (Mitroff & Pauchant, 1990; Coombs, 2012; Sellnow & Seeger, 2006). The focus on reputation and organizations leads us back to the area of communication studies and research on actors, stakeholders and communities (Fearn-Banks, 2016; Seeger, Sellnow, & Ulmer, 2003). Since the 1990s, crisis communication research has been slowly incorporated into nonprofit organizations. For instance, reputational crisis can influence operations in nonprofits, such as the American Red Cross and its history of questionable blood draw practices, management scandals and donation mismanagement after the September 11, 2001, terrorist attacks, and disjointed response to Hurricane Katrina (Sisco, Collins, & Zoch, 2010).

Theories of Crises and Communication

Theories focused on crises and communication are varied. One of the first concepts investigated regarding crisis and impending communication efforts was *focusing events* generated by Birkland (1996; 1997; 1998; 2006). Birkland spoke to the phenomena of natural disasters acting as focusing events for policy change. With each new disaster, a spotlight is given to the policies and procedures related to the disaster. For many policies, the question of how to prevent the disaster from happening again is posed along with how to improve policies that failed during response and recovery. Within these focusing events, leaders have a window of opportunity for change in terms of policies and regulations as the event opens up a communication channel. Birkmann et al. (2010) analyzed these windows of opportunity not only due to the impact they have on political, social and economic arenas, but on the ability for leadership to communicate and to frame focusing events. Although the perspective of focusing events and windows of opportunity are mainly connected to politics and agenda setting, these theoretical perspectives hinge on communication efforts by organizational leadership and the relationship with their communities (Birkland, 1996; 1997; 1998; 2006; Birkmann et al., 2010).

The next concept examined is *renewal discourse*. This discourse incorporates four theoretical objectives that highlight a crisis as an opportunity for organizational learning, ethical communication, prospective vision and positive rhetoric (Ulmer, Sellnow, & Seeger, 2007, 2017). In terms of organizational learning, the crisis unveils areas of growth, which is a similar concept to Birkland's focusing event and other researchers that see disasters as learning opportunities (Birkland, 2009; Drupsteen & Guldenmund, 2014; Norris et al., 2008; Perry & Nigg, 1985; Toft & Reynolds, 2016). The focus on *ethical communication* is to emphasize the organization's positive values that are, hopefully, in place before, during and after the crisis. These values range from honesty, transparency and trustworthiness and are the best predictors of *positive renewal*. Including a prospective vision means incorporating optimism into communication and keeping the organization's purpose and mission in mind to support renewal. The last concept of the discourse of renewal is *positive rhetoric* and connects to the leadership who would inspire others to stay committed to the cause. The discourse of renewal is seen to contrast corporate apologia or image restoration theory as not beginning from a perspective of protecting or repairing the organization's image (Ulmer, Sellnow, & Seeger, 2007, 2017). Albeit an idealistic approach, the reality of crises and disasters incorporates negatively impacted reputations and public images necessitating a restoration or repairing element.

An additional model for crisis communication is the Center for Disease Control and Prevention's Crisis and Emergency Risk Communication (CERC) lifecycle (2014). Although the focus is on public health and lends itself more toward the arena of risk communication, the model emphasizes six principles that connect to best practices of emergency management-related communication. These principles include being first, right, credible, empathic, action-oriented and respectful. The lifecycle of CERC is similar to the generalized timeline for emergency management related communication of pre-crisis, during and after with expansion to include an evaluation component. CERC also incorporates similarity to situational crisis communication theory with consideration for crisis type. However, the intricate focus on public health and lack of expansion to all areas of emergency management led to further theoretical evaluations (CDC, 2014).

Situational Crisis Communication Theory and Strategies

Linking crisis rhetorical theory and strategies with attribution theory, Coombs (2012) developed *situational crisis communication theory* (SCCT) to "evaluate the reputational threat posed by the crisis situation and then recommend crisis response strategies based upon the reputational threat level" (p. 138). The crisis response strategies came as a result of apologia, *impression management* and image restoration theory. The incorporation of attribution theory, a social science traditional framework, applies to crisis management situations by taking an audience-centered approach and considering the reaction of stakeholders to an event (Coombs, 2012). Attribution theory focuses on how an individual cognitively processes cause and effect within their environment (Kelley, 1967; Weiner, 1985). SCCT expands the concept from individual focused on an event to a group of individuals and how they infer a cause related to the action of an organization (Sellnow & Seeger, 2013; Ulmer, Sellnow, & Seeger, 2017; Walker, 2012). This is helpful for practitioners as SCCT takes into account an organization's reputation, types of crisis the organization may face and potential audience response to generate specific strategies to prevent or mitigate potentially negative impacts.

It is due to the nuances and uniqueness within SCCT that make it a relevant and useful theory for nonprofit leaders and organizations in their crisis communication efforts.

At the heart of SCCT is an emphasis on recovering from the crisis. It attempts to balance proactive and reactive measures in a way to intentionally respond and recover. With one of the overarching goals being to maintain a positive reputation within crisis response, SCCT is predominantly utilized in public relations research and acknowledges how the public will assign responsibility to response organizations (Sellnow & Seeger, 2013; Walker, 2012). More specifically, SCCT incorporates *attributional theory*, which focuses on the degree to which individuals or a stakeholder will hold an organization responsible for a crisis. A threat to effective communication consists of any negative reputation held by an administrator or organization. This theory proposed four groups of response strategies: Denial, Diminish, Rebuild and Bolstering (see below). The response strategies can assist nonprofit leaders in determining the overarching goal of their crisis communication efforts and the outcomes they desire. The basic premise holds that with the increase in attribution to an organization concerning crisis responsibility, strategies must be adapted to meet the increased needs.

1. Denial strategies – "Seek to prevent any connection between the organization and some crisis event and include denial, attacking the accuser, and scapegoating".
2. Diminish strategies – "Try to reduce the perceived responsibility for the crisis and include justification and excuses".
3. Rebuild strategies – "Attempt to improve the reputation and include compensation and apology".
4. Bolstering strategy – "Try to draw on existing goodwill and should be used as a secondary strategy in support of others" (Coombs, 2012, p. 11).

In terms of a starting off point for basic crisis communication strategies, a nonprofit leader can begin with a threat assessment of crisis type, history and prior reputation. The communication based crisis typologies include natural disasters, workplace violence, rumors, malevolence, challenges, technical-error accidents, technical-error product harm, human-error accidents, human-error product harm and organization misdeeds (see Table 3.1 for definitions). Understanding the differences in the types of internal and external crises an organization can face allows for more tailored responses.

Depending on typologies, nonprofit leaders will relate preparation, mitigation, response and recovery activities to previous events and gauge predilection for future events. Prior connections determine whether the community holds a negative or positive reputation for an organization's resilience capacity (Coombs, 2012; Reynolds & Seeger, 2005; Sherrieb, Norris, & Galea, 2010). In conjunction with the leader's response, the type of crisis impacts the communication needs and previous history, or experiences, will affect how emergency management practitioners and their community will respond (Coombs, 2012; Jin & Pang, 2012; Liu, Austin, & Jin, 2011; Reynolds & Seeger, 2005; Sherrieb, Norris, & Galea, 2010; Ulmer, Sellnow, & Seeger, 2017; Walker, 2012).

SCCT broadens these strategies and provides a prescriptive system to connect response strategies to the crisis situation (Coombs & Holladay, 2002). A nonprofit leader's response to a crisis directs the ability to adapt communication and whether they include community needs and vulnerable populations into this adaptation (see Table 3.2 for crisis response strategies) (Coombs, 1999; Coombs & Holladay, 2002; Sellnow & Seeger, 2013).

In addition to the response strategy groupings, SCCT takes into consideration crisis clusters, which were formed by integrating crisis type with attributions of crisis responsibility (Coombs, 2014; Coombs & Holladay, 2002).

Table 3.1 Definitions of Crisis Typologies

Crisis Type	Definition
Natural disasters	When an organization is damaged as a result of the weather or "acts of God" such as earthquakes, tornadoes, floods, hurricanes and bad storms
Workplace violence	When an employee or former employee commits violence against other employees on the organization's grounds
Rumors	When false or misleading information is purposefully circulated about an organization or its products in order to harm the organization
Malevolence	When some outside actor or opponent employs extreme tactics to attack the organization, such as product tampering, kidnapping, terrorism or computer hacking
Challenges	When the organization is confronted by discontented stakeholders with claims that it is operating in an inappropriate manner
Technical-error accidents	When the technology utilized or supplied by the organization fails and causes an industrial accident
Technical-error product harm	When the technology utilized or supplied by the organization fails and results in a defect or potentially harmful product
Human-error accidents	When human error causes an accident
Human-error product harm	When human error results in a defect or potentially harmful product
Organizational misdeeds	When management takes actions it knows may place stakeholders at risk or knowingly violates the law

Source: Coombs (2012).

1. Victim cluster – weak attributions of crisis responsibility where the organization is considered a victim. These include natural hazards, workplace violence, product tampering and rumor.
2. Accidental cluster – minimal attributions of crisis responsibility and the event is considered uncontrollable or unintentional by the organization. These include technical-error accidents, technical-error product harm and challenge.
3. Intentional/preventable cluster – strong attributions of crisis responsibility and the event is considered purposeful. These include human-error accident, human-error product harm and organizational misdeed.

Once the nonprofit leader understands the crisis type and the potential response strategies, messages can be crafted to meet the organization's needs and goals (see Table 3.3) (Coombs & Holladay, 2002; Ulmer, Sellnow, & Seeger, 2017).

Table 3.2 Crisis Response Strategies

Response Strategy	Description
Attack on the accuser	Crisis manager confronts the group or person that claims a crisis exists
Denial	Crisis manager claims that there is no crisis
Excuse	Crisis managers attempt to minimize organizational responsibility for the crisis
Victimization	Crisis manager reminds stakeholders that the organization is a victim of the crisis as well
Justification	Crisis managers attempt to minimize perceived damage inflicted by the crisis
Ingratiation	Crisis manager praises stakeholders and reminds them of the past good works done by the organization
Corrective action	Crisis manager tries to prevent a repeat of the crisis and/or repair the damage done by the crisis
Full apology	Crisis manager publicly accepts responsibility for the crisis and requests forgiveness from the stakeholders

Source: Adapted from Coombs (2012).

Crisis Communication Planning Framework

The question for many organizations when it comes to crisis communication planning is: Where to begin? Haupt and Azevedo (2021) conducted a search of current guides to crisis communication planning resulting in six documents that provided unique insights specific to the nonprofit sector. After analyzing the focused resources, Haupt and Azevedo (2021) created a crisis communication planning framework that incorporated recommendations from the resources along with the professional experience of the researchers.

A resource by Lenhoff-Briggs (2018) provides a ten-step process focused on crisis management and the reality that a crisis can occur at any time and that the worst thing that can occur is for a nonprofit to say nothing when chaos erupts. The overarching push is to be proactive versus reactive in nature. A guide by Shannon (2015) emphasized the difference between an issue versus a crisis as well as generating worst-case scenarios for the crisis types. An *issue* is a negative situation the organization must process, but it does not have a long-lasting impact on its operations or reputation. An issue can turn into a *crisis* if there is a long-lasting impact on the organization's operation or reputation. Examples include the UWA financial management crisis, the American Red Cross' problematic response during Hurricane Sandy and Isaac and numerous local-level nonprofits who faced reputational threats after financial mismanagement surfaced or inaccurate reporting of services rendered (Haupt & Azevedo, 2021; Norris 2015; Sisco, Collins & Zoch 2010).

Table 3.3 Crisis Type and Strategy Matching

Crisis Types		Crisis Response Strategies	
Victim cluster	Natural disaster	**Deny strategies**	Attack the accuser
	Rumor		Denial
	Workplace violence		Scapegoat
	Product tampering/ malevolence		
Accidental cluster	Challenges	**Diminish strategies**	Excuse
	Technical-error accidents		Justification
	Technical-error product harm		
Preventable cluster	Human-error accidents	**Rebuild strategies**	Compensation
	Human-error product harm		Apology
	Organizational misdeed with no injuries or with injuries or management misconduct		

Source: Adapted from Coombs (2012).

A resource by Ciesielka (2015) was more of a resource packet that included professional not-for-profit resources such as data collection and analysis organizations, educational organizations providing access to articles, journals and university collected crisis communication plans. A key takeaway, however, was Ciesielka's (2015) connection to social media monitoring technology and public relations tools and services to improve plans and strategies of organizations. The public relations focus allows organizations to identify objectives, target audiences, media contacts, consequences, top-tier audiences, credibility and expertise, monitoring, staffing, and inventory of public relations tools (Haupt & Azevedo, 2021).

New England Insurance Services (NEIS, n.d.) provided insights into the information gathering portion of crisis management when you are needing to answer the who, what, when, where, why, how and what now. In addition, NEIS (n.d.) speaks to the immediate aftermath of a crisis and the need to stabilize the situation and make sure everyone is ready to engage with the public and the media along with implementing crisis communication plans. It is an important moment of time to gather thoughts and resources before moving forward. Norris (2015) provided a key aspect of crisis communication planning and strategy implementation in communicating internally and externally. Organizations are better able to mitigate negative damage to their reputation and operation if they engage with external stakeholders early on and provide a cohesive message (Haupt & Azevedo, 2021; Norris 2015).

The Colorado Nonprofit Association (CNA, 2014) provided a template for nonprofit organizations to support their own development of a crisis communication plan and adapt it to their organization's resources, structures and messages. Another unique aspect of CNA's (2014) crisis communication plan is the policies concerning the plan and its implementation. Connecting to policies provides organizational support and showcases intentionality (Haupt & Azevedo, 2021). The review of the guides resulted in strategies that are listed in Table 3.4.

Haupt and Azevedo (2021) also generated a crisis communication planning framework based off of promoted strategies, emergency management communication practices and crisis communication literature (see Figure 3.1). Within this framework, recommendations are connected to *pre-crisis*, *crisis* and *post-crisis* time periods. Each time period incorporates best practices and aspects organizations need to accomplish for effective crisis communication planning and implementation.

> Essentially, if a nonprofit leader is aware of how they will respond to the crisis, then they are more apt to pick a strategy that will positively impact their company as they will tailor their messages and instruct specific stakeholders in such a way to circumvent any negative consequences.

In addition, knowing the strategies and promoted practices assists those receiving the information to understand how the nonprofit is viewing the crisis and how the organization and the community will be impacted by their leadership. The focus on governance and leadership is discussed in the next chapter and connects to the crisis communication planning framework in terms of communication specific roles and responsibilities during a crisis and understanding organizational context and attribution.

Summary of Key Points

- Situational crisis communication theory (SCCT) broadens communication strategies found in general emergency management and crisis communication practice by providing a prescriptive system to connect response strategies to the crisis situation integrated with adaptations for an organization's needs and crisis typology.
- General recommendations and considerations revolve around: (1) how to transfer the message; (2) when to send the message; (3) will the recipient see, read or hear the message; (4) is the message comprehensible; and (5) what will be the response.

Table 3.4 Crisis Communication Resources for Nonprofit Organizations

Source	Date	Strategies for Crisis Communication Planning
Colorado Nonprofit Association (CNA)	2014	1. Identify the purpose of the crisis communication plan 2. Identify who is to utilize the crisis communication plan 3. Generate policies based off of the plan and for implementation 4. Create a checklist that includes safety, notification, crisis communication team, steps to take before going public, what to do when going public, and evaluation of the efforts 5. Select persons to be part of the internal emergency phone tree 6. Strategically create the crisis communications plan to have internal pre-preparation, safety, notifications, a team, situational assessment, decision-tree matrix, key messages, staff notification, board and chair notification, media releases, partner and key group notification, record keeping, media-message evaluation, communications updates, loose ends, evaluations, and post-crisis clean-up
Compassion Capital Fund (CCF)	n.d.	1. Identify a hierarchy for the communication process 2. Generate key statements for stakeholders and media connections 3. Utilize crisis communication to supplement a risk management and response plan
Sean Norris from NonProfitPro Podcast	2015	1. Tell it all, tell it early 2. Have a plan 3. Determine what you would do if you were to the response before the crisis, during and after
Meg Shannon from Nonprofit MarCommunity	2015	1. Issue vs. crisis- know the difference 2. Create a worst-case scenario 3. Build your team 4. Have an escalation plan 5. Practice makes perfect 6. During the crisis: don't let it fester 7. Gather the facts 8. Craft a statement 9. Address the crisis where it happened 10. Take responsibility and forget about blame

(Continued)

Table 3.4 (Continued)

Source	Date	Strategies for Crisis Communication Planning

Tom Ciesielka of TC Public Relations	2015	1. Utilize professional not-for-profit resources
		2. Engage in online social media monitoring
		3. Utilize professional public relations tools and services
		4. Generate a public relations crisis planning worksheet encompassing:
		  • initial public relations objectives;
		  • target audience;
		  • target media contacts;
		  • consequences;
		  • top-tier audiences;
		  • credibility and expertise;
		  • monitoring;
		  • staffing; and
		  • inventory of public relations tools.
		5. Educate yourselves with public relations texts and resources and maintain a list of these resources

Allyssa Lenhoff-Briggs	2018	1. Identify your crisis communications team 2. Anticipate possible problems and crisis 3. Identify spokespeople 4. Identify audiences 5. Establish notification systems 6. Create foundational statements 7. Assess the crisis 8. Create crisis-specific messaging 9. Monitor systems 10. Analyze after the crisis
New England Insurance Services	n.d.	1. Generate action steps 2. Gather information 3. Contacting emergency services 4. Determine ways to stabilize the situation 5. Identify crisis headquarter locations 6. Prepare a script 7. Create a contact sheet 8. Mobilize a crisis team 9. Determine emergency and support sources 10. Media management tips 11. Identify post-incident follow-up 12. Create a crisis response kit 13. Organize files and prepare reports 14. Have a Plan B 15. Engage in self-care

Non-Crisis Period

Identify a Planning Team → Crisis and Risk Identification → Communication Strategy Formulation → Designation of Roles and Responsibilities → Selection of organizational Resources to Support Strategies → Communication with Internal and External Stakeholders → Training and Practice

Crisis Period

Identify the Crisis → Identify impact to Organization → Select Spokesperson → Refer to applicable Strategies → Invest Organizational Resources for Response Efforts → Communicate with Internal and External Stakeholders → Maintain Records of all Communication Strategies Utilized → Note Initial Impact

Post-Crisis

Collet After-Action Reports → Evaluate Internal Impact of Crisis Communication Strategies → Evaluate External Impact of Crisis Communication Strategies → Incorporate Results of Assessment and Evaluation into Crisis Communication Plans → Incorporate Results of Assessment and Evaluation into Organizational Politics ad Procedures

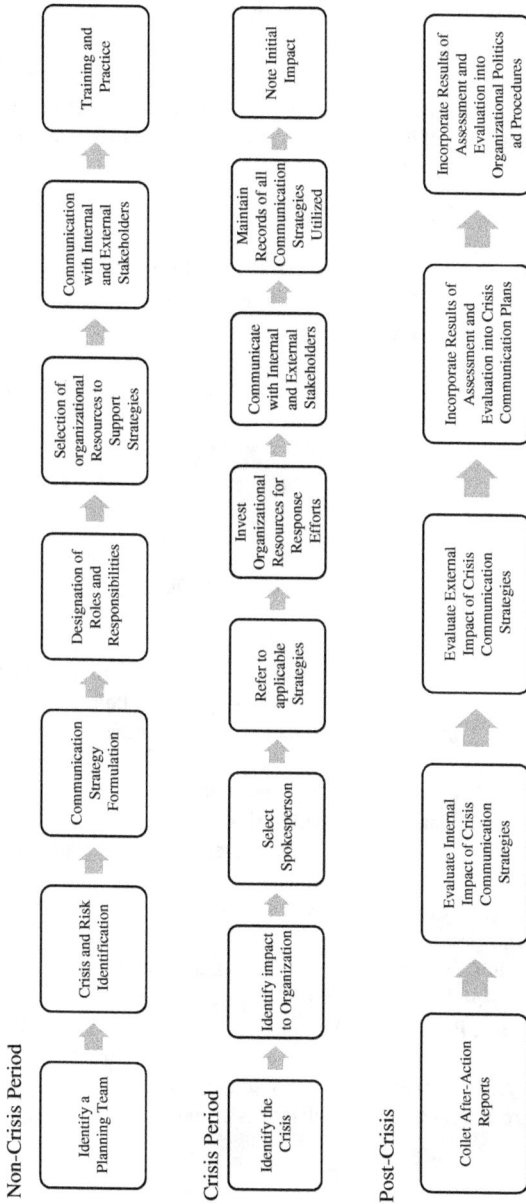

Figure 3.1 Crisis Communication Planning Framework.

- In terms of basic crisis communication strategies, an administrator or emergency manager can begin with a threat assessment of crisis type, history and prior reputation. The typologies include natural disasters, workplace violence, rumors, malevolence, challenges, technical-error accidents, technical-error product harm, human-error accidents, human-error product harm and organization misdeeds.
- At the heart of SCCT is an emphasis on recovering from the crisis. More specifically, SCCT is focused on the degree to which individuals or a stakeholder will hold an organization responsible for a crisis.

Discussion Questions

1. What are aspects to consider for crisis communication?
2. How do apologia and restoration theory impact crisis communication?
3. What types of crises are there?
4. What types of basic response strategies are there?
5. What are the strategies found within situational crisis communication theory?

References

Allison, G. T. (1971). *Essence of decision: Explaining the Cuban Missile Crisis.* Boston: Little Brown.

Almond, G. A., Flanagan, S. C., & Mundt, R. J. (Eds.). (1973). *Crisis, choice, and change: Historical studies of political development.* Boston: Little Brown.

Birkland, T. A. (1996). Natural disasters as focusing events: Policy communities and political response. *International Journal of Mass Emergencies and Disasters, 14*(2), 221–243.

Birkland, T. A. (1997). *After disaster: Agenda setting, public policy, and focusing events.* Georgetown University Press: Washington, D.C.

Birkland, T. A. (1998). Focusing events, mobilization, and agenda setting. *Journal of Public Policy, 18*(1), 53–74.

Birkland, T. A. (2006). *Lessons of disaster. Policy change after catastrophic events.* Georgetown University Press: Washington, DC.

Birkland, T. A. (2009). Disasters, lessons learned, and fantasy documents. *Journal of Contingencies and Crisis Management, 17*(3), 146–156.

Birkmann, J., Buckle, P., Jaeger, J., Pelling, M., Setiadi, N., Garschagen, M., ... & Kropp, J. (2010). Extreme events and disasters: A window of opportunity for change? Analysis of organizational, institutional and political changes, formal and informal responses after mega-disasters. *Natural Hazards, 55*(3), 637–655.

Boin, A., & McConnell, A. (2007). Preparing for critical infrastructure breakdowns: The limits of crisis management and the need for resilience. *Journal of Contingencies and Crisis Management, 15*(1), 50–59.

Center for Disease Control and Prevention. (2014). *Crisis and emergency risk communication: An introduction.* Retrieved from https://emergency.cdc.gov/cerc/ppt/CERC_Introduction.pdf.

Chandler, R. C. (2010). *Emergency notification.* ABC-CLIO: Santa Barbara, CA.

Ciesielka, T. C. (2015). *Crisis communications for not-for-profits resource guide.* TC Public Relations. Retrieved from https://www.tcpr.net/wp-content/uploads/2015/10/TCPR-Nonprofit-Reputation-Resource-Guide.pdf.

Coombs, W. T. (1999). Information and compassion in crisis responses: A test of their effects. *Journal of public relations research, 11*(2), 125–142.

Coombs, W. T. (2012). *Ongoing crisis communication: Planning, managing, and responding.* Sage Publications: Oxford, United Kingdom.

Coombs, W. T., & Holladay, S. J. (2002). Helping crisis managers protect reputational assets initial tests of the situational crisis communication theory. *Management Communication Quarterly, 16*(2), 165–186.

Diesing, P. (1992). *How does social science work?: Reflections on practice.* University of Pittsburgh Press: Pittsburgh, PA.

Drupsteen, L., & Guldenmund, F. W. (2014). What is learning? A review of the safety literature to define learning from incidents, accidents and disasters. *Journal of Contingencies and Crisis Management, 22*(2), 81–96.

Fearn-Banks, K. (2016). *Crisis communications: A casebook approach.* Routledge: Oxfordshire, United Kingdom.

Flin, R. (1996). *Sitting in the hot seat: Leaders and teams for critical incident management: Leadership for critical incidents.* Chichester: John Wiley & Sons Ltd.

George, A. L. (1991). *Avoiding war: Problems of crisis management.* Westview Press: Boulder, CO.

Haupt, B., & Azevedo, L. (2021). Crisis communication planning and nonprofit organizations. *Disaster Prevention and Management: An International Journal, 30*(2), 163–178.

Herek, G. M., Janis, I. L., & Huth, P. (1987). Decision making during international crises is quality of process related to outcome? *Journal of Conflict Resolution, 31*(2), 203–226.

Hermann, C. F. (Ed.). (1972). *International crises: Insights from behavioral research.* Free Press: New York, NY.

Jin, Y., & Pang, A. (2010). Future directions of crisis communication research: Emotions in crisis–The next frontier. In Timothy, Coombs & Sharry, Holliday (Eds.), *Handbook of crisis communication* (pp. 677–682). Blackwell Publishing: Oxford, England.

Kapucu, N., Hawkins, C. V., & Rivera, F. I. (Eds.). (2013). *Disaster resiliency: Interdisciplinary perspectives.* Routledge: Oxfordshire, United Kingdom.

Kapucu, N., & Özerdem, A. (2011). *Managing emergencies and crises.* Jones & Bartlett Publishers: Burlington, MA.

Keeler, J. T. (1993). Opening the window for reform: Mandates, crises, and extraordinary policy-making. *Comparative Political Studies, 25*(4), 433–486.

Kelley, H. H. (1967). Attribution theory in social psychology. In *Nebraska symposium on motivation*. University of Nebraska Press: Omaha, NB.

Klein, G. A. (1999). *Sources of power: How people make decisions*. MIT Press: Cambridge, MA.

Lebow, R. N. (1984). *Between peace and war: The nature of international crisis*. Johns Hopkins University Press: Baltimore, MD.

Lenhoff-Briggs, A. (2018). *Ten steps for effective crisis management for nonprofit organizations*. Retrieved from https://www.rjweanfdn.org/wp-content/uploads/2018/02/02.22.18-Crisis-Communications-Plan-VS.-FINAL-1.pdf.

Linz, J. J., & Stepan, A. (1978). *The breakdown of democratic regimes: Europe (Vol. 2)*. John Hopkins University Press: Baltimore, MD.

Liu, B. F., Austin, L., & Jin, Y. (2011). How publics respond to crisis communication strategies: The interplay of information form and source. *Public relations review, 37*(4), 345–353.

McEntire, D. A. (2007). *Disaster response and recovery: Strategies and tactics for resilience*. New Jersey: Wiley.

Mitroff, I. I., & Pauchant, T. C. (1990). *We're so big and powerful nothing bad can happen to us: An investigation of America's crisis prone corporations*. Birch Lane Press.

Norris, S. (2015). *Crisis management: how two nonprofits handled crisis- why you should be prepared*. NonProfitPro Podcast. Retrieved from https://www.nonprofitpro.com/article/crisis-management-how-two-nonprofits-handled-crisis-and-why-you-need-to-be-prepared/all/.

Norris, F. H., Stevens, S. P., Pfefferbaum, B., Wyche, K. F., & Pfefferbaum, R. L. (2008). Community resilience as a metaphor, theory, set of capacities, and strategy for disaster readiness. *American Journal of Community Psychology, 41*(1–2), 127–150.

Perry, R. W., & Nigg, J. M. (1985). Emergency management strategies for communicating hazard information. *Public Administration Review, 45*, 72–77.

Reason, J. (1990). *Human error*. Cambridge University Press: Cambridge, MA.

Reynolds, B., & Seeger, M. W. (2005). Crisis and emergency risk communication as an integrative model. *Journal of Health Communication, 10*(1), 43–55.

Rosenthal, U., Boin, A., & Comfort, L. K. (2001). *Managing crises: Threats, dilemmas, opportunities*. Charles C Thomas Publisher: Boca Raton, FL.

Seeger, M. W. (2006). Best practices in crisis communication: An expert panel process. *Journal of Applied Communication Research, 34*(3), 232–244.

Sellnow, T. L., & Seeger, M. W. (2013). *Theorizing crisis communication (Vol. 4)*. John Wiley & Sons: Hoboken, NJ.

Seeger, M. W., Sellnow, T. L., & Ulmer, R. R. (2003). *Communication and organizational crisis*. Greenwood Publishing Group: Westport, CT.

Shannon, M. (2015). How to create a crisis communication plan for your nonprofit. Nonprofit MarCommunity. Retrieved from https://nonprofitmarcommunity.com/crisis-communications-plan/.

Sherrieb, K., Norris, F. H., & Galea, S. (2010). Measuring capacities for community resilience. *Social Indicators Research, 99*(2), 227–247.

Sisco, H. F., Collins, E. L., & Zoch, L. M. (2010). Through the looking glass: A decade of Red Cross crisis response and situational crisis communication theory. *Public Relations Review, 36*(1), 21–27.

Smith, K. B., & Larimer, C. W. (2016). *The public policy theory primer.* Westview Press: Boulder, CO.

Stern, E. (1997). Crisis and learning: A conceptual balance sheet. *Journal of Contingencies and Crisis Management, 5*(2), 69–86.

Sylves, R. (2014). *Disaster policy and politics: Emergency management and homeland security.* CQ Press: Washington, D.C.

Toft, B., & Reynolds, S. (2016). *Learning from disasters.* Springer: New York, NY.

Ulmer, R. R., Seeger, M. W., & Sellnow, T. L. (2007). Post-crisis communication and renewal: Expanding the parameters of post-crisis discourse. *Public Relations Review, 33*(2), 130–134.

Ulmer, R. R., Sellnow, T. L., & Seeger, M. W. (2017). *Effective crisis communication: Moving from crisis to opportunity.* Sage Publications: Oxfordshire, United Kingdom.

Walker, D. C. (2012). *Mass notification and crisis communications: Planning, preparedness, and systems.* CRC Press: Boca Raton, FL.

Waugh, W. L., & Streib, G. (2006). Collaboration and leadership for effective emergency management. *Public Administration Review, 66*(s1), 131–140.

Weiner, B. (1985). An attributional theory of achievement motivation and emotion. *Psychological Review, 92*(4), 548.

4 Governance Strategies and Leadership during Crises

Lauren Azevedo

Nonprofit Governance and Executive Leadership

Nonprofit leadership and governance is an intricate, dynamic and complex interdependent relationship (Chait et al., 2011; Heimovics et al., 1993) The rapport between the board of directors and the executive director is an important resource for nonprofits as it can leverage the organization's mission and help increase *social capital* (King, 2004; Miller & Bergman, 2008).

Social capital includes social resources incorporating aspects such as relationships, norms, trust and values (Coleman, 1990). Cultivating these relationships and building trust is strategic work focused on increasing organizational effectiveness (Brown, 2000; Miller-Millensen, 2003).

During crisis times, a balance between the board of directors and executive leadership activities and responsibilities is required. Nonprofit executives face specific challenges in working with the board to fulfill the mission, resource acquisition and strategy. Executive directors and board members should separately ask themselves how they are collectively meeting responsibilities to define and refine the mission. At times, the executive director and board of directors may face muddy waters in terms of how their partnership works, especially during a crisis or when something goes wrong in the organization. Often, people are inclined to blame others, perhaps due to the self-serving hypothesis (Heimovics, Herman, & Coughlin, 1993), by making illogical attributions in an effort to protect themselves, their reputation and identity or their ego.

A sound governance structure with a working and effective relationship between the board of directors and executive director is imperative to the nonprofit's mission, vision, values and goals.

DOI: 10.4324/9781003147480-4

Governance Strategy Examples

An abundance of nonprofit literature is devoted to understanding governance structures that nonprofits may follow or adapt. For instance, Houle's (1997) *tripartite model of governance* is often used as a comprehensive and interactive model for nonprofits. Within this model are three integral parts: the executive director, board of directors and staff. The focus of the board is on the organization's mission and engaging in strategic planning to ensure mission congruence with activities (Houle, 1997). Good governance behaviors and activities include mission congruence and setting policies, selecting and monitoring the executive director, approving long-range organizational plans, overseeing programs to ensure objectives are met, securing financial resources and integrating the organization with its environment. There is shared responsibility between the executive director and the board, though in most cases, the board is the legally dominant partner. It is the executive director's responsibility to teach the staff about the board and ensure that staff members understand the challenges and complexities of the board–executive–staff relationship (Houle, 1997).

Worth (2016) suggests John Carver's *governance model*, as well as Chait and his colleagues' (2011) *governance as leadership model*, are often utilized in nonprofit organizations. The cornerstone of Carver's model is the redefinition of policy and the policymaking process. The policy model has four main policies that all other policies fall under: ends, executive limitations, board management delegation and the governance process (Carver & Carver, 2006). There are critiques of applying Carver's model to small nonprofit organizations, those in financial trouble or that require a strong, supportive board because of their phase of development or complexity (Bradshaw, 2009). Additionally, the model is critiqued for being prescriptive and theoretical rather than practical (Bradshaw, 2009). However, there are capacity building practices and policies that have implications for nonprofit organizational effectiveness and can be beneficial in certain types of crises.

The governance as leadership model addresses critical issues facing the organization by sharing leadership between the executive director and the board (Worth, 2016). In this model, trustees and executives are given a new framework to help govern their organizations effectively by enhancing the board's value to the organization (Chait et al., 2011). The emphasis of this model is on leadership and encourages trustees to think like managers. Three types of governance are emphasized in the governance as leadership model: fiduciary, strategic and generative (Chait et al., 2011). Together, Chait and his colleagues identify executives as enabling effective trusteeship. The model places much emphasis on governing in the generative mode, as this is the most neglected governance mode yet the most important type of work that a board may do and maximum benefit can be acquired.

Contingency Approach to Governance

According to Brown (2000) different governance models may prove to be effective, but they should reflect organizational needs and environmental constraints.

Some research suggested nonprofit organizations develop their own board model to follow based on the organization's environment, history, personalities and culture (Brudney & Murray, 1997). Research by Bradshaw (2009) and Ostrower and Stone (2010) suggests that a *contingency approach* can provide useful and insightful facilitation and rethinking of current governance practices in nonprofit organizations. The contingency approach to board governance allows organizations to reframe challenges to a more impersonal, structural or sociological view as opposed to a view where people involved in challenges were the cause of the problem. Four governance configurations within the contingency approach policy, constituency/representative, entrepreneurial/corporate and emergent cellular by Bradshaw (2009) are presented in Figure 4.1 along with their key features. Organizations in uncertain environments may use entrepreneurial/corporate or emergent cellular while policy and constituency/representative governance may be more appropriate in stable environments. Other organizations may use a hybrid of one of these governance structures, depending on their context and strategic decisions.

McMullin and Raggo (2020) apply Bradshaw's (2009) four governance configurations to the COVID-19 pandemic, a community technical crisis.

Policy	Constituency/ represnetative	Entrepreneurial/ corporate	Emergent cellular
• Formalized • Traditional	• Decentralized • Designed for responding to different stakeholders	• Focus on efficiency and planning	• Organic • Flexible • Much less formalized

Figure 4.1 Key Features of the Contingency Governance Approach by Bradshaw (2009).

Their work suggests governance configurations designed for stable environments will be more impacted in their activities, while board configurations designed to adapt in turbulent environments will have less interruption in their management activities (McMullin & Raggo, 2020). These findings provide implications for governance in crisis management.

Being prepared for contingencies within the board and understanding crisis stages and response, good governance strategies may pivot to include temporary committees, additional meetings or streamlined voting procedures during crises.

This leadership structure may be less responsive to interruptions and better able to account for crisis planning in various environments.

What Is a Good Board? Who Is a Good Board Member?

In general, there are group-level indicators of board performance (Herman, Renz, & Heimovics, 1997; Holland & Jackson, 1998) and individual indicators of board member performance (Brown, 2007; Preston & Brown, 2004).

A good board provides advice and accountability and understands the mission well enough to set clear and appropriate strategic objectives. Strong boards understand the importance of networking and building effective relationships and recognize its members and stakeholders as valuable organizational assets.

Holland and Jackson (1998) identify six key board competencies essential for effective governance:

1. Contextual competence, or understanding and accounting for organization's context
2. Educational competency, or ensuring steps necessary for sharing information about the organization
3. Interpersonal competence, or nurturing development and capacities of the group
4. Analytical competency, or recognizing complex issues and using multiple resources to develop appropriate responses
5. Political competency, or ensuring healthy communications between stakeholders
6. Strategic competency, or envisioning the direction for a strategic approach for the future (Holland & Jackson, 1998)

These competencies have been useful for creating self-assessments of boards in subsequent studies and in practice (Azevedo, 2021; Gill, Flynn, & Reissing, 2005; Lichtsteiner & Lutz, 2012; Mannion et al., 2017; Marberg, Korzilius, & van Kranenburg, 2019).

On the individual level, board members should have certain expertise that fits in well with the organization's activities or mission, add diversity to the board, have used the services of the organization, understand the service community well, expand the organization's network and/or bring in social capital to the organization. Good board members bring in *board capital*, defined as the human, structural and social capital that individuals bring to the board to facilitate success (Azevedo, 2021). A "good" board member does not look exactly the same for every organization or every position.

In addition to less effective board members, 'bad' board members also exist. Board members who do not attend meetings, who attend meetings but do not participate, who do not add to the diversity, expertise or capital to the board or who are uninformed of the organization's mission, vision and values may negatively impact the organization. They pose a risk of endangering their organization and may contribute to crises or negative reputation. These members are at risk of personal liability and intermediate sanctions may need to be executed. One established way of getting rid of weak board members includes setting board term limits in addition to regular self-assessments of board performance.

The Power of the Board of Directors

Board power is a very important, yet often a neglected, part of nonprofit governance (Bradshaw, Murray, & Wolpin, 1992). Boards hold the power to hire and fire executive directors, allocate resources, vote on programs and projects, assign volunteers, create committees for special programs, make decisions on partnerships and collaborations, apply for grants and innovate the organization, among many other roles and privileges. *Resource dependency theory* gives attention to the board's boundary spanning role and responsibility and shows how power and influence have the capacity to bias resource allocation decisions in nonprofit organizations (Miller & Millesen, 2003). Beyond resource allocation, attracting powerful board members can increase organizational effectiveness (Miller & Millesen, 2003) and influence decisions during crises. *Board power* culminates in having strong board members with potential to implement specific actions and influence stakeholders.

Several other theories guide the foundation of board power, responsibility and risk assessment, including agency theory, stakeholder theory and managerial hegemony. These theories provide insight into how leaders understand, plan, lead and develop organizational policies applicable to crises. *Agency theory*, for instance, can help resolve issues between principals and agents and enhance relationships among stakeholders through effective communication and matched objectives (Miller, 2002). The theory suggests shareholder wealth and organizational performance are maximized when a board of directors monitors the chief executive's tendency to behave with self-interest. Agency theory has been applied widely to study the board of directors to better understand monitoring and behavior of the board.

Stakeholder theory provides implications on management and ethics for constituencies impacted by organizational entities (such as staff or volunteers). In crises, nonprofit leaders must make decisions in complex environments of heterogeneous and competing stakeholder claims, where judgment of stakeholder power must be considered when making organizational decisions (Willems, 2020). Critical aspects of the theory are that leaders prioritize stakeholders based on their respective power and the role of individual leaders is critical, as they play an active part in managing stakeholder relationships acting as mediators between stakeholders and organizational decisions (Willems, 2020). Agency and stewardship theories have investigated governance and accountability in nonprofits and are an effective tool to examine a single nonprofit organization where the board of directors has the primary responsibility for ensuring that governance functions are carried out.

Often the relationship with a particular stakeholder group of the nonprofit organization is hierarchical, so one party expects another party to perform some service on its behalf. *Managerial hegemony theory* assumes the board's power is limited and control is given to the managers of the organization. Consequently, managers will make strategic decisions that will fit their objectives (Raeymaekers, 2020). Power within a board may also be limited and may negatively impact organizational effectiveness. Mace (1971) states managerial hegemony "claims that due to the largely voluntary nature of board members' involvement and the subsequent constraints on their time, board power is limited and control is ceded to the managing director and his or her staff" (p. 119).

Representing the Organization and Crisis Leadership

Nonprofit leaders, including board members, have the responsibility of representing their organization to the public. This requires certain skills in working with public agencies, the media and presentations to internal and external stakeholders, even if the leader is not the organization's designated spokesperson or crisis communication coordinator. Technology is important in communicating, making computer and language skills important to ensuring the nonprofit is meeting the public's high standards of excellence. *Media communications* are also very important, meaning nonprofit leaders should be able to communicate the organization's mission, vision and goals, as well as operations and programming. In addition to external relationship skills, nonprofit leaders must develop skills in listening to stakeholders and community members. This is important for involving stakeholders in decision-making and building relationships to grow their network.

Leaders in crisis may turn to literature on the topic of crisis leadership due to the complexity surrounding diverse responsibilities in addition to complex crisis situations (Gajewski et al., 2011). The literature is scant on understanding nonprofit crisis leadership and how leaders make sense of crisis. *Crisis sensemaking*, or how leaders and other organizational representatives understand the crisis situation and provide organizational responses, has received little attention in the nonprofit sector. Gilstrap et al. (2016) sought to investigate this knowledge gap. The sensemaking phenomenon for leaders in crisis is worthy of study given what we know of studying sudden changes within organizational groups that upend routines and other conditions within an organization leading to difficult and stressful organizational responses (Weick, 1988).

> Findings from Gilstrap et al. (2016) suggest that while several leadership qualities are important for effective crisis leadership, the following six are particularly important: (1) team player; (2) strategic; (3) transparent with stakeholders; (4) quick to respond; (5) self-composed; and (6) prepared.

Nonprofits leaders in their study found that certain frameworks were important in the sensegiving process during crises. These included instrumental knowledge, meaning leading with consistent and important organizational information and using that knowledge to diagnose and comprehend the crisis, lead constituents to crisis understanding and formulate a response. A second framework that was found to be important was Normalcy. Normalcy incorporates leaders who could spin the crisis as an urgent but normal, expected event within the organization, which can not only help calm fears but also make it seem like the organization may be prepared for such a situation. The final framework that was found to be important for leadership sensemaking in crisis is dynamic learning, meaning leaders can craft crisis response in ways that suggest learning is important and they will respond better to problems by learning from the past so that the crisis is not as significant or detrimental in the future (Gilstrap et al., 2016).

General Board Responsibilities

The board holds much accountability and leadership in nonprofit organizations.

The board is accountable to the community, the state, clients and beneficiaries and encompasses four general types of responsibilities, including: governance and strategic direction, resource development and acquisition, support of staff, and monitoring and oversight (Renz, 2016).

More specifically, core board functions include leading the organization, establishing policies, securing resources, hiring and managing the executive director, engaging with partners, ensuring accountability, and ensuring board and organizational effectiveness (Renz, 2016).

Boards also have legal responsibilities to their organizations, including the *duty of care, duty of loyalty* and *duty of obedience* (Renz, 2016). The duty of care means making good judgment on decisions, or one that a prudent person may make under similar circumstances. Board members should be diligent and attentive and consider laws and decisions that impact the

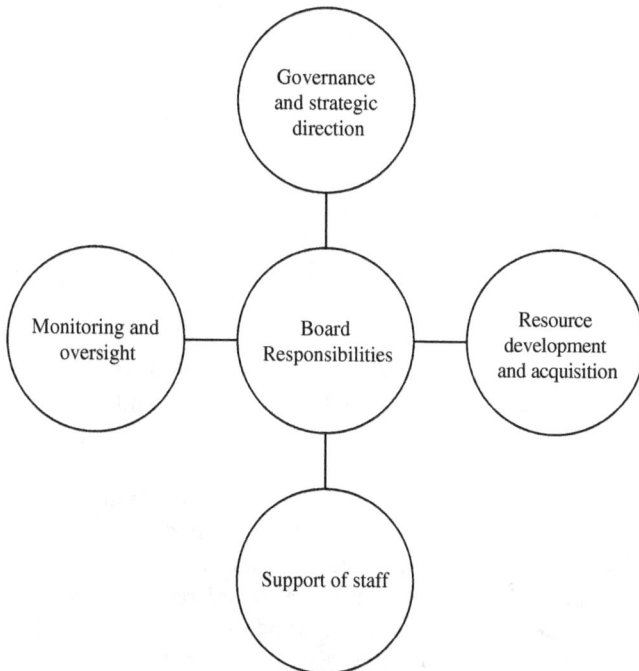

Figure 4.2 Board Responsibilities.

organization. The duty of loyalty requires boards to act in good faith for the best interest of the nonprofit. The duty of obedience means that board members should adhere to the mission, bylaws and policies, as well as standards of appropriate behavior, in their actions. Boards also have a fiduciary responsibility, typically surrounding: policies for resource acquisition, establishing a budget, monitoring staff and volunteers, monitoring and assessing fiscal performance of the nonprofit and using an external review process regularly (such as an audit).

There are instances when board members can be held personally liable, mostly surrounding employment practices. These may include: when conflict of interest policies are violated and when the board violates contracts. This may also occur when the board fails to take responsible steps to avoid harm and puts individuals, including staff, volunteers or other stakeholders, at risk.

Nonprofits and Risk Management

The Nonprofit Risk Management Center (2015) defines risk management as "a discipline that can help you understand the risks you face, modify your behavior accordingly and prepare your nonprofit to thrive in an uncertain future".

> *Risk management* is a process of ascertaining an organization's legal, financial and reputational risks and actively working to avoid them.

It often includes having appropriate policies and procedures in place to manage the organization's finances, employees, volunteers, service recipients and ensuring the proper governance. Nonprofit leaders assume risk management responsibilities in their positions and should work diligently to plan to minimize potential risks in their organization.

> The practice of good risk management enables nonprofits to focus on their mission and service delivery and maintain trust while avoiding potential lawsuits (Herman, 2016).

Nonprofits should have a risk management committee, consisting of individuals that have broad organizational knowledge, in addition to knowledge on day to day risks faced by the organization (Herman, 2011). Such a committee should have staff representation, board representation, an attorney and other outside professionals to guide the organization. The committee should be in charge of active risk management. This involves three steps, according to the Public Counsel Law Center (2013), including: (1) assess risk by identifying actions and relationships that could go wrong; (2) mitigate risk by considering what needs to be done to prevent accidents from happening, including physical precautions and administrative procedures; and, (3) insure for risk by procuring insurance for the organization.

During crisis situations, nonprofits must keep in mind all risks associated with the organization, including their service populations. Often these include vulnerable populations, such as the youth, elderly, low-income groups and/or individuals with developmental disabilities. They should also ensure management of risks associated with these populations as they may not be able to advocate for themselves. Additionally, nonprofits should consider risks associated with their volunteers, which are a unique consideration from other sectors.

Nonprofit organizations need to protect volunteers from the effects of accidents and injuries, both planned and unplanned. Often volunteers lack health, accident and disability insurance; therefore, their activities within the organization could cause significant financial risks for a nonprofit. To address such risks, organizations should ensure proper fit between organization and responsibilities with volunteers, provide specific safety training, guarantee safety communication and messaging is clear between staff and volunteers, consider providing first aid training for volunteers working events with community members and conduct incident response planning so there is a protocol in place if something goes wrong at a volunteer event.

Cybersecurity is another area of risk for nonprofits and should be included in risk management activities. Cybersecurity means taking steps to protect critical systems, operations and information from digital attacks from inside or outside of an organization. Activities related to cybersecurity may include appropriate resources allocated to information technology infrastructure, appropriate security measures and training, procedures for password maintenance and security and appropriate security software in place for monitoring sensitive data. Cybersecurity protocols, in addition to adequate safety training, incident planning and insurance are vital risk management procedures for nonprofit organizations.

Expanding the risk management focus to crisis communication, nonprofit organizations also need to prepare for diverse crises. The communication based crisis typologies include natural hazards, workplace violence, rumors, malevolence, challenges, technical-error accidents, technical-error product harm, human-error accidents, human-error product harm and organization misdeeds. Review Chapter 3 for more details.

Summary of Key Points

- Boards contribute to organizational crisis response in unique ways. During crisis times, a balance between the board of directors and executive leadership activities and responsibilities is required.
- Nonprofit literature well explores examples of governance structures that nonprofits may follow or adapt. Houle's (1997) tripartite model of governance, Carver's governance model (2006) and Chait et al.'s (2005) governance leadership model are examples of different governance structures that a nonprofit can employ.
- Recent work suggests a contingency governance approach may work well for organizations' unique situations and certain configurations within such an approach may be helpful for organizations in uncertain, or crisis, environments.
- Whatever the governance structure, the board of directors should work closely with the executive and assume important responsibilities and accountability, including the organization's governance and strategic direction, resource development and acquisition, supporting staff and monitoring and oversight of the organization.
- Agency theory, stakeholder theory and managerial hegemony theory all provide insight into board roles, responsibilities and power dynamics. Individual nonprofit leaders must represent their organization well to the public and ensure they are equipped with important communication and leadership skills.
- During crises, effective leadership means being strategic, working well with others, being transparent, responding quickly, remaining composed and being prepared. When boards are not well prepared or do not follow set policies or contracts, it puts the organization at risk.
- Risk management committees can help assess, mitigate and insure against risks.

Discussion Questions

1. What are the considerations for an appropriate governance structure?
2. How can a nonprofit organization recruit leaders that respond well in crisis situations?
3. What are the board's legal responsibilities?
4. Why is a risk management committee important?

Additional Resources

Janssen, M., & Van Der Voort, H. (2020). Agile and adaptive governance in crisis response: Lessons from the COVID-19 pandemic. *International Journal of Information Management*, 55, 102180.

References

Azevedo, L. (2021). Board capital and board effectiveness: An examination of Florida community foundations. *Journal of Nonprofit Education and Leadership*. https://doi.org/10.18666/JNEL-2021-10775

Bradshaw, P. (2009). A contingency approach to nonprofit governance. *Nonprofit Management and Leadership*, *20*(1), 61–81.

Bradshaw, P., Murray, V., & Wolpin, J. (1992). Do nonprofit boards make a difference? An exploration of the relationships among board structure, process, and effectiveness. *Nonprofit and Voluntary Sector Quarterly*, *21*(3), 227–249.

Brown, W. A. (2000). *Organizational effectiveness in nonprofit human service organizations: The influence of the board of directors*. The Claremont Graduate University: Claremont, CA.

Brown, W. A. (2007). Board development practices and competent board members: Implications for performance. *Nonprofit Management and Leadership*, *17*(3), 301–317.

Brudney, J. L., & Murray, V. (1997). Improving nonprofit boards: What works and what doesn't. *Nonprofit World*, *15*(3), 11–17.

Carver, J., & Carver, M. (2006). *Reinventing your board: A step-by-step guide to implementing policy governance* (Vol. 18). John Wiley & Sons: Hoboken, NJ.

Chait, R. P., Ryan, W. P., & Taylor, B. E. (2011). *Governance as leadership: Reframing the work of nonprofit boards*. John Wiley & Sons: Hoboken, NJ.

Coleman, J. S. (1990). *Foundations of social theory*. Cambridge, MA: Harvard University Press.

Cornforth, C. (2012). Nonprofit governance research: Limitations of the focus on boards and suggestions for new directions. *Nonprofit and Voluntary Sector Quarterly*, *41*(6), 1116–1135.

Gajewski, S., Bell, H., Lein, L., & Angel, R. J. (2011). Complexity and instability: The response of nongovernmental organizations to the recovery of Hurricane Katrina survivors in a host community. *Nonprofit and Voluntary Sector Quarterly*, *40*(2), 389–403.

Gill, M., Flynn, R. J., & Reissing, E. (2005). The governance self-assessment checklist: An instrument for assessing board effectiveness. *Nonprofit Management and Leadership*, *15*(3), 271–294.

Gilstrap, C. A., Gilstrap, C. M., Holderby, K. N., & Valera, K. M. (2016). Sensegiving, leadership, and nonprofit crises: How nonprofit leaders make and give sense to organizational crisis. *VOLUNTAS: International Journal of Voluntary and Nonprofit Organizations*, *27*(6), 2787–2806.

Heimovics, R. D., Herman, R. D., & Coughlin, C. L. J. (1993). Executive leadership and resource dependence in nonprofit organizations: A frame analysis. *Public Administration Review, 53*(5), 419–427.

Herman, M. L. (2011). *Ready... or not: A risk management guide for nonprofit executives.* Nonprofit Risk Management Center.

Herman, M. L. (2016). Risk management. In David O. Renz & Robert D. Herman (Eds.), *The Jossey-Bass handbook of nonprofit leadership* (2nd edition, pp. 560–584). San Francisco, CA: John Wiley & Sons: Hoboken, NJ.

Herman, R. D., Renz, D. O., & Heimovics, R. D. (1997). Nonprofit organizations. *Nonprofit Management & Leadership, 7*(4).

Houle, C. O. (1997). *Governing boards: Their nature and nurture.* San Francisco, CA: Jossey-Bass.

Jackson, D. K., & Holland, T. P. (1998). Measuring the effectiveness of nonprofit boards. *Nonprofit and Voluntary Sector Quarterly, 27*(2), 159–182.

King, N. K. (2004). Social capital and nonprofit leaders. *Nonprofit Management and Leadership, 14*(4), 471–486.

Lichtsteiner, H., & Lutz, V. (2012). Use of self-assessment by nonprofit organization boards: The Swiss case. *Nonprofit Management and Leadership, 22*(4), 483–506.

Mace, M.L. (1971). *Directors: Myth and reality.* Boston: Harvard Business School Press.

Mannion, R., Davies, H. T. O., Jacobs, R., Kasteridis, P., Millar, R., & Freeman, T. (2017). Do hospital boards matter for better, safer, patient care? *Social Science & Medicine, 177*, 278–287.

Marberg, A., Korzilius, H., & van Kranenburg, H. (2019). What is in a theme? Professionalization in nonprofit and nongovernmental organizations research. *Nonprofit Management and Leadership, 30*(1), 113–131.

McMullin, C., & Raggo, P. (2020). Leadership and governance in times of crisis: A balancing act for nonprofit boards. *Nonprofit and Voluntary Sector Quarterly, 49*(6), 1182–1190.

Miller, B. S., & Bergman, J. (2008). Developing leadership on boards of directors. *Journal for Nonprofit Management, 12*(1), 2–58.

Miller, J. (2002). The board as a monitor of organizational activity: The applicability of agency theory to nonprofit boards. *Nonprofit Management & Leadership. 12*(4), 1–15. Retrieved from https://onlinelibrary-wiley-com.ezaccess.libraries.psu.edu/doi/epdf/10.1002/nml.12407.

Miller-Millesen, J. L. (2003). Understanding the behavior of nonprofit boards of directors: A theory-based approach. *Nonprofit and Voluntary Sector Quarterly, 32*(4), 521–547.

Nonprofit Risk Management Center. (2015). *What is risk?* Retrieved from http://www.nonprofitrisk.org/about/mission.html.

Ostrower, F., & Stone, M. M. (2010). Moving governance research forward: A contingency-based framework and data application. *Nonprofit and Voluntary Sector Quarterly, 39*(5), 901–924.

Preston, J. B., & Brown, W. A. (2004). Commitment and performance of nonprofit board members. *Nonprofit Management and Leadership, 15*(2), 221–238.

Public Counsel Law Center. (2013). *A nonprofits guide to risk management and insurance.* Los Angeles, CA: Retrieved from https://www.publiccounsel.org/wp -content/uploads/2021/12/Risk-Management-Insurance-Guide-for-Nonprofits -2013.pdf.

Raeymaekers, P. (2020). The governance of public - nonprofit service networks: Four propositions. *Nonprofit and Voluntary Sector Quarterly, 4*(2), 3–10.

Renz, D. O. (2016). Leadership, governance, and the work of the board. In David O. Renz & Robert D. Herman (Eds.), *The Jossey-Bass handbook of nonprofit leadership and management* (4th edition, pp. 127–166). John Wiley & Sons.

Weick, K. E. (1988). Enacted sensemaking in crisis situations [1]. *Journal of Management Studies, 25*(4), 305–317.

Willems, J. (2020). In the name of the stakeholder: As assessment of representation surpluses and deficits by nonprofit leaders. *Nonprofit Management & Leadership, 3*(2), 2–8. Retrieved from https://onlinelibrary.wiley.com/doi/full/10.1002/nml .21445.

5 Preparing for Crisis Communication Planning

Brittany "Brie" Haupt

Introduction

Preparing for the crisis communication planning process is as intentional as any strategic planning process. Setting aside the time, resources and talent to engage in this endeavor is critical as planning assists in organizational growth and development. The outcome of crisis communication planning, for organizations in any sector, is mitigating potential negative impacts to the organization, supporting growth and development, and enhancing and justifying public value through organizational mandates and fulfillment of public service initiatives. This outcome can only be accomplished by tying together the mission, vision, goals, decisions and management. More importantly, crisis communication planning is not a one-size-fits-all type of process because it must account for a diverse range of organizations, each with different implementation and organizational structures. These diverse organizations are part of the complex infrastructure of the United States, which has a population of more than 333 million people (National Center of Charitable Statistics, 2019; United States Census Bureau, 2021). Imagine trying to satisfy the needs of the public and provide essential services without strategically planning each endeavor and anticipating risks and negative impacts to operation and reputation. The concept of strategic planning and the diversity of methods surfaces again when engaging in the process and implementing each facet.

Importance of a Crisis Communication Plan

Organizational crisis involves great uncertainty (Lerbinger, 1997). Ray (1999) suggests the more the uncertainty, the higher the severity of the crisis. When a crisis happens, communication needs are immediate. Questions during crises regarding cause, blame, resolution and consequences influence organizational uncertainty and make it important for organizations to strategize communications in their plan for dealing with various environments

DOI: 10.4324/9781003147480-5

(Ray, 1999; Stephens et al., 2005). With a solid plan dealing with communications, nonprofits are better situated to respond and resume operations as quickly as possible, while maintaining their reputation and donors.

Planning during non-crisis times is essential. In fact, planning is the first step in overcoming the crisis. Crisis communication plans are a key component for organizational preparedness and strategy. Not having a crisis communication plan can cost a nonprofit its reputation, donors, staff, volunteers, collaborators, and ultimately, its programs and sustainability. A key part of crisis planning for nonprofits is consideration of stakeholders and how to reach different internal and external stakeholder groups through the crisis. The plan should detail all the steps that are followed along with pre-prepared organizational responses, messaging development, and information. When crises happen, these resources place the organization in a better position to get information out to stakeholders expeditiously. This allows for the time needed to brainstorm strategies, generate a crisis management organizational hierarchy, determine any resource or logistical needs, practice the plan with the organization's members as well as relevant community partners, collaborate with local emergency managers to check with the community's comprehensive emergency management plan and reduce duplication of efforts and identify any missing aspects, and to check with the nonprofit's legal team to determine any potential liabilities. All these aspects assist with building the *resilience capacity* of the organization and have the best chance to reduce or eliminate any negative impact to the organization (Haupt & Azevedo, 2021).

Initiating the Planning Process

Before initiating the planning process, the members of the planning committee need to set up an ideal environment and timeline. Many strategic planning initiatives occur during weekend retreats, weekly scheduled meetings, teleconferences and more. The planning environment and timeline depends solely on the organization's size, resource support and deadline. However, it is useful to set aside dedicated time for crisis communication planning and have the environment be conducive to planning efforts. For example, in-person planning should occur in spaces that are comfortable to the committee members and has access to technology, white boards, easels, organizational documents and basic necessities, such as restrooms and vending. If planning is to occur during a retreat, then the committee should take time to consider logistic arrangements and confirm access to organizational and educational documents if unable to log into the organization's technological infrastructure. If via teleconference then measures should be in place should the actual technology use become an issue with bandwidth and network connections. Though these logistical recommendations may seem common sense, nothing can impact the beginning of a planning process more than being in an environment where these considerations are nonexistent to the point that the efforts have to be deferred to another time period.

Range of Planning Models

There are a variety of strategic planning models, processes and matrices developed over time, such as the Harvard policy model, portfolio model, Ansoff matrix, performance measurement, balance scorecards, and the strategy change cycle (Bryson, 2004, 2018; Haupt, 2021). This list is not exhaustive; other models focus on collaboration, mix and matching models (hybrid models) and decision-making. Planning efforts and resources connected to planning models have historically focused on public and private sector operations. The impetus being financial stability and justifying public value to internal and external stakeholders. Although the emphasis is mainly economic, there are aspects of the planning models that relate to the nonprofit sector.

The Harvard policy model was developed in the 1920s and focused on how private firms fit best within their operational environment (Dolence, 2004; Haupt, 2021). The key component of this model was the creation of the SWOT analysis. By analyzing the internal (strengths and weaknesses) and external (opportunities and threats) environment, firms are more capable of fulfilling their social obligations. Although this model did not assist in generating strategies, it was the first to call attention to the intersection between internal and external environments.

During the 1950s, we saw the focus on capital budgeting and planning increasing into the development of portfolio models (Proctor & Hassard, 1990). These models focused on the financial relationship between supply and demand in conjunction with a firm's public value and stakeholder response. An example of a matrix utilized within the portfolio model is the Boston Consulting Group (BCG) matrix developed by Bruce Henderson. This matrix focused on categorizing firms into four distinct possibilities:

- High-growth/high-share firms that generate substantial revenue but require large investments to maintain or increase market share
- Low-growth/high-share firms that generate large revenue flows with low investment and utilize profits elsewhere
- Low-growth/low-share firms that produce little revenue and offer little prospect of increased share
- High-growth/low-share firms that require substantial investment in order to become high growth/high share or low growth/high share but with questionable investment

All this categorization allowed for a method to measure aspects of a firm that are of strategic importance. The difficulty is determining what exactly needs measurement, how to classify these aspects and how to integrate portfolio models into large strategic planning processes.

The need for a focus on decision-making led to the arena of strategic management. Still connected to business methods, economists and business administrators were searching for ways to integrate model results into decision-making processes (Haupt, 2021). From the 1960s to mid-1970s, scholars attempted to find a remedy for this situation, and one outcome was the Ansoff Matrix. This matrix assisted firms in decision-making through examination of risk to their bottom line.

The next overarching focus of strategic planning models was performance measurement to maximize quality of services and programs in a cost-effective manner and still achieve organizational mission, vision and goals (Haupt, 2021). Strategic planning and performance measurement were soon viewed as two sides of a coin. The strategic plan assists with identifying goals and achieving outcomes, while performance measurement provides critical feedback to keep the plan on target. Performance measurement became more of an emphasis in the public sector due to financial constraints and demands from the public. The balance scorecard is one example of how to measure performance and meet mandates (Sharma, 2009). A balanced scorecard is a strategic management performance metric that helps companies identify and improve their internal operations to help their external outcomes. It measures past performance data and provides organizations with feedback on how to make better decisions in the future.

The next aspect to tackle is how to integrate strategic planning into strategic management. Bryson (2004, 2018) developed the strategy change cycle as a strategic management process used to link planning and implementation and ensures that strategic management is an ongoing process. The ten-step process is a cyclical strategic change process and should be seen as very fluid, iterative and dynamic in practice. It also allows for a reasonably orderly, participative and effective approach to determining how to achieve what is best for an organization. The ten steps are as follows (Bryson, 2018):

1. Initiate and agree on a strategic planning process.
2. Identify organizational mandates.
3. Clarify organizational mission and values.
4. Assess the external and internal environments to identify strengths, weaknesses, opportunities and threats.
5. Identify the strategic issues facing the organization.
6. Formulate strategies to manage the issues.

7. Review and adopt the strategic plan or plans.
8. Establish an effective organizational vision.
9. Develop an effective implementation process.
10. Reassess strategies and strategic planning process.

Within these models, the first step is to determine how the planning process will proceed. Many scholars discuss how success can be achieved if an organization does the following:

- Identify and communicate the need for change.
- Provide a plan (a course of action or strategy for implementing change).
- Build internal support and overcome resistance.
- Ensure support and commitment from top management.
- Build external support.
- Provide adequate resources to support the change process.
- Institutionalize change.
- Develop an integrative, comprehensive approach that achieves subsystem congruence.

Identifying Organizational Attributes

Before creating the initial agreement, it is critical to identify organizational attributes within the strategic planning process. Attributes, defined below, include the organization's purpose, strategies, goals, mandates, objectives, core values/beliefs and stakeholders. In essence, by identifying an organization's attributes, the planning committee is able to determine the organization's culture and capabilities.

- The *vision* statement is the overarching idea of what the organization is trying to accomplish.
- The *mission* statement is the general idea of how the vision will be achieved.
- *Goals* include general statements of how to achieve the various strategies that were created to support the mission statement.
- *Mandates* include legislative or financial aspects an organization needs to achieve for funding purposes or to meet specified stakeholders' expectations.
- *Objectives* are specific milestones the organization is attempting to reach and create its definition of success.
- An organization's *core values/beliefs* outline its philosophical lens and thereby direct all its actions.

- *Stakeholders* are those entities invested in the organization's success. Stakeholders impact or are impacted by the strategic plan.

Mandates and missions are the most efficient way to showcase how the organization is socially justified and seen as a legitimate endeavor. These aspects are the basis of an organization's public value. This is not as simple as it sounds. Each organization, regardless of sector, has a social contract with the society it operates within. These mandates, whether formal or informal, are how an organization achieves support and legitimacy. If an organization can accomplish these mandates, then its public value increases; conversely, if an organization fails to accomplish these mandates, then it is at risk of being deemed illegitimate and may find itself losing support and funding.

In tandem with organizational mandates, it is imperative to identify and clarify an organization's mission. While some enter a chicken or an egg debate on which area should come first – mandates or mission – what is important is to understand how mandates and missions connect with each other. By identifying organizational attributes, an organization is better able to understand the planning environment and reacquaint itself with its purpose and basic operations.

The Initial Agreement

The initial agreement is a formal document among the crisis communication planning committee that establishes how a strategic plan will be created (Bryson, 2004, 2018). Essentially, you strategically plan the crisis communication plan. It will cover the following:

- The purpose and worth of the effort
- The stakeholders involved
- Steps to be followed and decision-making structure
- Timeline for reports and benchmarks
- Roles and responsibilities
- Commitment of resources
- Leadership support
- Conflict resolution

Establishing these aspects guides the planning process and provides a stronger foundation for when crises occur. Justification of the crisis communication planning process begins with understanding the *purpose and worth of the effort*. The purpose of crisis communication planning can be focused on enhancing the reputational capital of the organization or supporting the organization's operations. The purpose can also revolve around mitigating liabilities to the organization or bouncing back from a negative event to prevent a future occurrence.

Identifying stakeholders is also critical to the initial agreement. As discussed in Chapter 1, a stakeholder is an individual or entity that impacts or is impacted by the organization. Once the planning committee has identified then a *stakeholder analysis* can be conducted to determine how the interests of those stakeholders should be incorporated into the planning process (Brugha & Varvasovszky, 2000; Bryson, 2004, 2018). For example, understanding the interests of internal and external stakeholders could lead to you including specific departments of the organization on the planning committee. In addition, the analysis can assist in determining which stakeholders are impacted most by specific crises so you can make specified circumvention strategies during the crisis communication planning process. For this initial agreement stage of the process, the important portion of the stakeholder analysis is to determine the make-up of the planning committee.

A stakeholder analysis can be completed by:

1. making a list of all internal and external stakeholders;
2. prioritizing stakeholders through power and interest grid (Bryson, 2004, 2018; see Figure 5.1); and
3. determining how to engage and communicate with stakeholders.

Power	High	High power, low interest	High power, high interest
		Keep these stakeholders satisfied, but they are not the main priority in terms of interest in the planning outcomes	You must fully engage these stakeholders, and make the greatest efforts to satisfy them
		Low power, low interest	Low power, high interest
	Low	Keep these stakeholders in mind, but they are not a priority for the planning process	Inform these stakeholders and keep them in communication to ensure that no major issues are arising
		Low	High
		Interest	

Figure 5.1 Power and Interest Grid Example.

In terms of *steps to be followed and the decision-making process*, this is where the committee establishes a preliminary idea of which planning processes the committee will undertake. In addition, the authority structure is discussed in terms of how decisions will be reached, who will manage the planning process and where to report results and communicate progression.

The next aspect to discuss is the *timeline* for the planning committee and potential outputs. Although the timeline may be altered as the planning process progresses, it is essential to have a preliminary idea of the timeline so those involved will understand the time commitment and the organization can anticipate when implementation, training and policies are expected to take place.

The next facet to discuss is the *roles and responsibilities* the committee will undertake. Who will lead the charge? Who will be responsible for communicating with internal and external stakeholders? Who is responsible for maintaining documentation? Who will perform any necessary training or generate policies? These are just a few of the aspects to discuss and then incorporate in the initial agreement so everyone knows their role and what they are responsible for.

The *commitment of resources* is the next to consider. Does the planning committee have a budget? Do they have access to the organization's resources? Do they have access to external funding? Are they able to hire talent specifically to assist the crisis communication planning process? How about funds for promotional materials?

Leadership support is another critical aspect to discuss. Success of a crisis communication plan depends on leadership supporting the process and the outputs. Leadership cannot support the process in name only, but they must be willing to commit resources and their own time. They also must engage in any necessary training and support accountability efforts for when policies and plans are implemented.

Conflict resolution is the final discussion of the initial agreement. This is where accountability is discussed along with how the committee members will handle any conflicts that arise. The conflicts could include timeline delays, work quality, personality clashes and much more. It is best to have this potentially uncomfortable discussion at the forefront of the planning process so that any negative impacts can be worked through more efficiently or even circumvented completely.

Completing and signing off on the initial agreement lays the foundation for the crisis communication planning process and sets the stage for success. In addition, the initial agreement proves useful when conflicts occur or the committee finds the need to justify its existence to organizational entities.

Summary of Key Points

- The outcome of crisis communication planning, for organizations in any sector, is mitigating potential negative impacts to the organization, supporting growth and development, and enhancing and justifying public value through organizational mandates and fulfillment of public service initiatives.
- Organizational attributes include the organization's purpose, strategies, goals, mandates, objectives, core values/beliefs and stakeholders. Identifying an organization's attributes allows you to understand the organization's culture and capabilities.
- The initial agreement guides the planning process and provides a stronger foundation for when crises occur.

Discussion Questions

1. What are the goals of crisis communication planning?
2. Why do you have to strategically plan to complete a crisis communication plan?
3. What are the aspects of an initial agreement?
4. Why are stakeholders so important to the process?
5. How can you conduct a stakeholder analysis?
6. Why is conflict resolution important to discuss in an initial agreement?

References

Brugha, R., & Varvasovszky, Z. (2000). Stakeholder analysis: A review. *Health Policy and Planning, 15*(3), 239–246.

Bryson, J. M. (2004). What to do when stakeholders matter: Stakeholder identification and analysis techniques. *Public Management Review, 6*(1), 21–53.

Bryson, J. M. (2018). *Strategic planning for public and nonprofit organizations: A guide to strengthening and sustaining organizational achievement.* Hoboken: John Wiley & Sons.

Dolence, M. G. (2004). The curriculum-centered strategic planning model. *Research Bulletin, 10*, 1–11.

Haupt, B. (2021). *Government, industry, and strategic planning: Course notes and documents (canvas course).* Richmond: Virginia Commonwealth University.

Haupt, B., & Azevedo, L. (2021). Crisis communication planning and nonprofit organizations. *Disaster Prevention and Management: An International Journal, 30*(2), 163–178.

Lerbinger, O. (1997). The crisis manager: Facing risk and responsibility (book review). *Journalism and Mass Communication Quarterly, 74*(3), 646.

National Center for Charitable Statistics. (2019). *The nonprofit sector in brief.* Retrieved from https://nccs.urban.org/project/nonprofit-sector-brief.

Proctor, R. A., & Hassard, J. S. (1990). Towards a new model for product portfolio analysis. *Management Decision, 28*(3).

Ray, S. J. (1999). *Strategic communication in crisis management: Lessons from the airline industry.* Greenwood Publishing Group.

Sharma, A. (2009). Implementing balance scorecard for performance measurement. *ICFAI Journal of Business Strategy, 6*(1), 7–16.

Stephens, K. K., Malone, P. C., & Bailey, C. M. (2005). Communicating with stakeholders during a crisis: Evaluating message strategies. *The Journal of Business Communication (1973), 42*(4), 390–419.

United States Census Bureau. (2021). *United States population.* Retrieved from https://www.census.gov/popclock/

6 The Crisis Communication Plan and Strategy Development

Lauren Azevedo and Brittany "Brie" Haupt

Elements of the Crisis Communication Plan

A nonprofit crisis communication plan is a strategic blueprint for the nonprofit to follow in case of an emergency or unexpected crisis. Crisis communication plans will look different for nonprofits depending on their size, location, stakeholders, community, programs and activities; however, there are some key features that all plans should have, including (1) purpose and overview of the plan; (2) an explanation of how to use the plan; (3) details of the crisis team; (4) a written crisis communication policy; (5) a list of potential or foreseeable crisis; (6) a list of stakeholders; (7) prepared messages and materials; (8) an emergency phone tree (for internal use); (9) a detailed crisis communication plan; (10) a list of communication channels; (11) a decision tree for actions and considerations; and (12) an after-crisis review plan. Each of these components is explored in more detail further.

Purpose and Overview

The purpose of the plan and its intended use should be clearly detailed in the beginning of the document (CNA, 2014; Haupt & Azevedo, 2021; Lenhoff-Briggs, 2018). The plan will also state where it should be stored and who has copies. A copy should be accessible by organizational leaders (including Board members) and should be stored at all organizational offices as well as somewhere off site and online so that it can be accessed by internal stakeholders. The overview will also detail the sections of the plan. A table of contents is useful for users.

The crisis communication coordinator should ensure that the crisis team has a copy of the plan, and its contents are updated regularly. The plan should note that the crisis team will review the plan on a regular basis (monthly, quarterly, annually, etc.). During the review of the plan, contact lists should be updated, new programs and risks are assessed and included, and any

DOI: 10.4324/9781003147480-6

Table 6.1 Example of Revision Table

Revision Date	Reviser Name	Approved Granted By	Notes on Changes

changes in policies and procedures should be revisited to ensure they are up to date. Each time changes are made, the crisis communication coordinator should note the updates and time of updates, as seen in Table 6.1.

Explanation of How to Use the Plan

The explanation may begin with defining a crisis and what the plan is, and then stating why the plan is significant for the organization and how it should be used. A thorough crisis communication plan can help speed up communication and ensure stakeholder safety and reputation management. The plan may include a set of objectives that will be addressed that can explain how and why to use the plan. This may include the following objective list, tailored to meet the needs of the organization:

- To form a crisis communication team and designated responsibilities
- To have a list of contact information for the crisis team and decision-makers
- To form a process for communicating with stakeholders
- To ensure stakeholder safety during and after a crisis
- To develop a process for informing stakeholders of decisions
- To manage stakeholder communications
- To identify various potential crisis and develop worst case scenarios
- To prepare a communications plan for the news, social media and other information platforms
- To help make decisions on how to act in various crisis situations
- To preserve organizational reputation
- To ensure communication systems exist for navigating various crisis situations

The Crisis Team

For crisis communication planning, it is essential to know who should be involved. Identifying the *crisis team*, or those responsible for organizational response to crisis, should be one of the first parts of the crisis communication plan. The plan should outline exactly who is involved and what their

Decision maker	Attorney	Crisis communication coordinator

Message developer	Emergency response liaison	Communication specialist

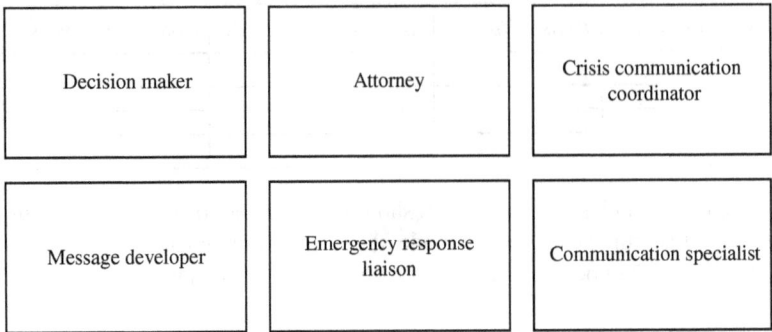

Figure 6.1 Crisis Team Features.

roles and responsibilities are before, during and after the crisis. Depending on the size of the nonprofit, the crisis team may only include the executive director, the board chair and executive leadership team. If the organization is larger, the crisis team may also include members of the marketing and communications team, the risk management team, the volunteer manager or representative and human resource representatives, among others.

The crisis team should also have at least one member with important key features, as seen in Figure 6.1. These include a decision-maker, who is often the executive director, who can make important decisions on behalf of the organization. An attorney is also an important person to include on the team in case the organization needs legal counsel, depending on the crisis and change in organizational operations during the crisis. A crisis communication coordinator ensures that clear information is given to both internal and external stakeholders. A message developer is responsible for coming up with the communication to share, based on the organization's mission and priorities, the established communication plan and the crisis team's decisions. An emergency response liaison is the designated person who speaks with law enforcement, emergency services and government officials as needed during crises. Finally, a person who is seasoned in communication strategies and can consult with inquiries and questions is a valuable crisis team member (Ciesielka, 2015; CNA, 2014; Lenhoff-Briggs, 2018; NEIS, n.d.).

The crisis team section of the crisis communication plan should outline who is in charge during the crisis and who is the organization's spokesperson. This includes who will speak to internal and external stakeholders, who will speak and respond to the press and who will manage email questions and social media accounts through the organization's social media platforms. While general message development can be shared by organizational leaders, everyone involved with the organization should be aware of who the spokesperson(s) are and should direct specifically questions to these individuals to ensure consistency and accuracy in messaging.

The crisis team's roles and responsibilities are important. They are responsible for planning for various types of crises and creating the crisis communication plan. Throughout the crises, they should ensure the plan is followed and carry out their respective roles. In addition, they are responsible for evaluating the plan after a crisis and determining what changes should be made to deal with future crises.

A Written Crisis Communication Policy

The crisis communication policy should include details of what needs to be done quickly before going public (CNA, 2014). This includes understanding and assessing the crisis, reiterating who is on the crisis team and determining who is responsible for each task, ensuring the designated crisis communication coordinator is available and can be the spokesperson, mitigating the crisis if possible, informing the staff and other stakeholders of the current situation and coming up with answers to questions that are likely to be asked.

Generally, nonprofits should have a pre-crisis communication guide set up in case of crisis situations that include a 24-hour phone tree, a password-protected webpage for internal stakeholders, an email or text alert system or a recorded phone call system. A constituent list and notification process table can help identify best practices in various crisis situations, as seen in Table 6.2. Depending on the nonprofit and its services, this will include vendor and supplier lists that may be impacted in different crisis scenarios.

Crisis communication plans should include a clear stepwise order of operation policy for immediately after a crisis happens. This is particularly important if the crisis was completely unforeseen, and the organization finds itself without a relevant plan during a crisis. Figure 6.2 shows a crisis communication overview of what to follow for any planned or unplanned crisis event.

Organizations also need to determine the most appropriate channels for communication during and after the crisis. A press release may or may not be necessary, depending on the crisis type and organization. In general, the

Table 6.2 Stakeholder Notification Process

Crisis Type	Stakeholder List	Process for Notification

Ensure site safety. Call 911, if necessary.	→	Notify the executive director and crisis coordinator.	→	Convene the crisis team.	→	Get internal affairs in order (before going public)

Communicate with critical audiences, including staff, board, and stakeholders.	→	Begin media outreach and press releases, if necessary.	→	Update website, voicemails, and social media accounts.	→	Assess messaging and communication as crisis unfolds.

Send post-crisis communication	→	Evaluate crisis communication efforts and update plan.

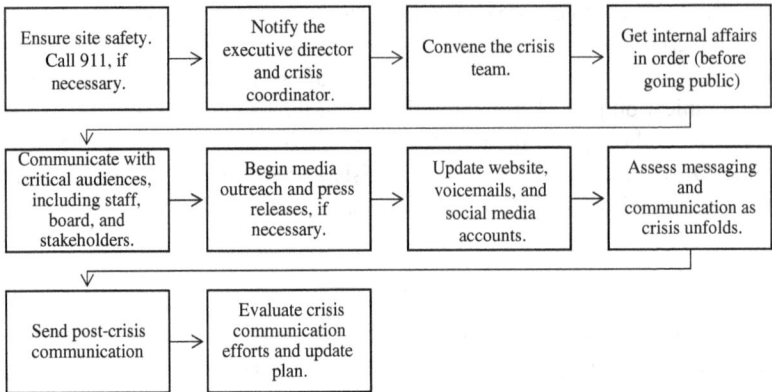

Figure 6.2 Crisis Communication Overview.

typical platforms used to share information are a good place to start (social media, email, website updates, etc.) (Ciesielka, 2015).

Pausing regular communications that are not crisis related when a crisis happens is an important part of the organization's crisis communication policy. This means stopping social media posts, web and email marketing campaigns and any other regular communications to focus on the crisis. This shows stakeholders that the organization understands that there is a crisis and is focusing on the situation. It also shows consideration for potential crisis victims.

A List of Potential or Projected Crises

As organizations begin identifying potential threats and organizational crises, difficult vulnerabilities may come to light that should be considered during planning (Shannon, 2015).

While the COVID-19 pandemic is still fresh in the minds of all organizations, many other types of crises can occur. Earthquakes, fires, active shooters, financial scandals, product recalls, fatal accidents at work, etc. This list likely recalls many other crises organizations can face and it can be quite daunting. The crisis team should take ample time brainstorming all potential crises the organization can face (refer to Chapters 1 and 3 on crisis types and strategies). Once an exhaustive list of potential crises is made, the crisis team should begin to consider how each crisis would be best handled, including steps that can be made now to limit impact and liability. Although this can be daunting, having a step-by-step list of each potential crisis type, along with details to consider through the crisis, will help when an actual crisis does occur. A list of potential crisis situations within the crisis communication plan may look something like Figure 6.3.

List of Stakeholders

A detailed list of stakeholders must be included in the crisis communication plan. As identified in the initial agreement, the stakeholder analysis is critical at this step as the power and interest grid will assist in determining priority of communication along with potential impacts by and to the stakeholders. More information regarding stakeholder communication is listed in Chapter 7.

Prepared Messages and Materials

Stakeholders will look for immediate and decisive organizational action. As soon as the crisis team is ready to go public, an initial statement should be communicated with the major crisis details (who, what, when, where). It is vital to ensure the information shared is accurate, the mission remains clear and the organization is concerned for crisis victims and stakeholders. As more information is known about the crisis, additional prepared messages should be made by the crisis communication coordinator. Anticipating possible messages is an important consideration for crisis communication plans. The crisis communication plan should have prepared message examples and materials included for each crisis type. Though they will vary significantly, during a crisis this is an excellent place for the crisis team to begin in formulating organizational responses. The organization's mission and goals should be a key part of the messaging that is shared. The messages should be practiced within the crisis team through crisis simulations.

The crisis communications team will be responding to the media and other stakeholder inquiries. While general messages may be drafted in the communications plan, they should be tailored to the crisis. Questions in Figure 6.4 help with *situational assessment* and should be anticipated in the initial communication.

In some crisis types, a command center may be necessary. The crisis communication plan should detail when a command center is necessary for the organization and what should be included in those instances. At a minimum, this may include copies of the communication plan with key contact information and resources, computers, internet and phones available, media contact lists and emergency supplies. Responsibilities should be designated to the command center responders, along with general messaging for crisis type and stakeholder. These messages will be tailored by the crisis team depending on the exact crisis. Creating a frequently asked questions (FAQs)

The nonprofit crisis team has identified the following scenarios that could impact the reputation, operations, or stability of this organization, including:

Organizational Technical Crises

- Failure of technology
  - o Phones offline
  - o Website down
  - o Internet down
  - o Computer crash
  - o Electricity out
  - o Heater/AC malfunction
- Service accident
- Confidentiality breech
- Failed fundraising plans or campaigns
  - o Does not meet goal
  - o No one shows up
  - o Does not cover costs
- Resource insecurity
  - o Lost grant
  - o Lost funder
  - o Increased rent
- Mission drift

Organizational Social Crises

- Workplace violence
- Injury at work
- Failure in communication
- Human error
- Poor board governance
- Poor staff or volunteer management or oversight

Community Technical Crises

- Natural disaster
  - o Tornado
  - o Hurricane/Tropical Storms
  - o Lightening
  - o Flooding
  - o Wildfire
  - o Earthquake
  - o Drought
- Government crisis
  - o Government shutdown
  - o Constitutional Crisis
  - o War declaration
- Disease outbreak
- International crisis

Community Social Crises

- School shooting
- Domestic terrorism
- International terrorism
- Sabotage
- Staff strike
- Volunteer strike
- False rumors
- Rogue volunteers

Figure 6.3 Identified Potential Crisis Situations.

What happened?	Where did it happen?	When did it happen?	Who did it happen to?

What caused the crisis?	Were there injuries	What is the safety plan?	How will future crisis be prevented?

	Who is in charge?	Is there a representative at the crisis site?	

Figure 6.4 Questions to Ask during Statement Drafting.

list is helpful for creating consistent messaging if multiple staff are working at the command center.

An Emergency Phone Tree (for Internal Use)

Before a crisis occurs, all internal stakeholders (including the Board, staff, and volunteers) should have an up-to-date *phone tree* and contact list that holds organizational leadership and the crisis team contact information (names, cell phones, home phones, addresses, email, etc.). The crisis team should ensure information is always up to date. Additional community emergency response resources should also be included on the list, such as police, fire, rescue, poison control, local hospitals, animal control, local police departments, water company, power company, partner organizations phone numbers, neighboring business phone numbers, tow truck number, insurance numbers, local emergency medical services, State Division of Wildlife, coast guard and any others that may be relevant.

An Easily Accessible Crisis Communication Plan

A detailed crisis communication plan begins with identifying crisis specific strategies and then classifying the strategies based on projected impact of the crisis. As discussed in previous chapters, there are several crises an organization will face. They could include operational or reputational, they can revolve around a natural, technological or civil/conflict hazards.

Organizations may classify the crisis level based on intensity, such as minimally intensive situations, moderately intensive situations or highly intensive crisis situations, as seen in Figure 6.5. Minimal intensive crisis situations include those that do not receive external attention. Moderately

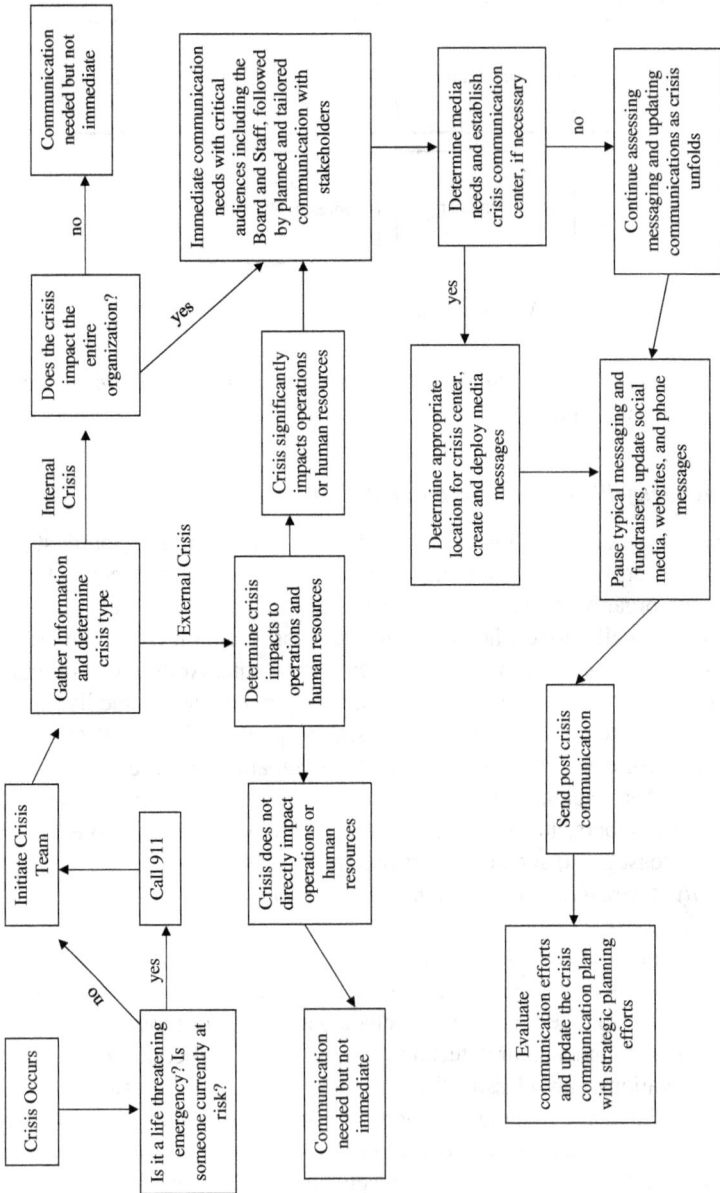

Figure 6.5 Decision Tree for Actions and Considerations.

intensive crisis situations suggest that the public are aware, but little attention is given to the crisis. Media may have inquiries to the organization, but attention is slow. In highly intensive crisis situations, there is an urgent need for communication, some individuals or groups may show anger or outrage, and/or there may be a crisis site that requires presence from the organization.

Nonprofits must remember when crises happen to respond as quickly as possible. Having potential strategies already created assists in reducing the reactivity time of an organization. Of course, this means ensuring the appropriate steps are happening so that the organization can remedy the situation in an informed and timely manner. It is appropriate to not have an answer to media or stakeholder questions immediately, but to follow up as soon as the crisis team has the information to assess an appropriate organizational response. It is critical to remain honest and sincere, showcasing the organization's commitment to addressing the situation within typical platforms (news media, newsletters, website, social media, etc.). It is appropriate to correct misinformation, but not to delete comments (particularly on social media). This suggests that the organization may be hiding or covering up a story when there is not one. To develop the crisis team, the communication plan may include a communications checklist (see Table 6.3).

Communication Channels

With diversity increasing across communities and stakeholders, cross-cultural communication is important to consider. It is essential to consider the diversity of stakeholders that nonprofits may serve, which could influence language and communication modes. With the increase in global diversity,

Table 6.3 Communications Checklist

_____	Notify and assemble the crisis team and assign duties as necessary
_____	Collect factual information on the crisis;
	Send designated crisis team member to crisis site if necessary (media spokesperson, researcher, subject matter expert, communications coordinator)
_____	Determine the crisis type (emergency level), severity, safety implications and timeline (one-time event, repeat event or ongoing crisis)
_____	Identify all stakeholder groups as well as any crisis victims
_____	Implement the appropriate communications strategy in the appropriate communications mechanism (social media, press release, website, etc.) using the pre-developed messages scaled to the crisis
_____	Develop materials for the press
_____	Inform stakeholders
_____	Continual assessment and evaluation

cross-cultural communication is only becoming increasingly important. Nonprofit leaders are increasingly engaging with diverse stakeholders and must recognize that adjustments may need to be made to operate effectively in a cross-cultural context. Cultural competence capacity can be defined as behaviors, attitudes and policies that work together in an organization to work effectively in diverse cultural situations (Denhardt, Denhardt, & Aristigueta, 2016; Stephens et al., 2005).

In terms of communication channels, organizations cannot rely on emails or social media campaigns to disseminate information. They must determine the availability of communication channels and which are best suited for the crisis. Communication channels can include:

- Telephone notification
- National Oceanic and Atmospheric Association Radios
- Email
- Social networking
- Text messaging system
- Commercial radio stations
- Local television stations
- Outdoor warning sirens
- Distributing flyers where/when needed
- Community website (e.g., surge zone, evacuation route maps, shelters)
- Daily situation reports made available online and through mass emails
- Press conferences
- Electronic signage

Decision Tree for Actions and Considerations

A decision tree helps organizations decide potential actions and guides decision-making based on various considerations that are important to the organization. The organization can create a decision tree during plan development on various platforms (Microsoft Word, PowerPoint, Viseo or any other visual software) to be used to help the crisis team when a crisis occurs. The decision tree can help in brainstorming solutions, exploring options and coming up with a consensus for communication needs, and typically incorporates important components of the crisis plan timeline. A decision tree example is showcased in Figure 6.5.

An After-Action Crisis Review

Organizations should ensure that there is a monitoring system in place to continually review the crisis and its impacts. Monitoring may not be necessary in all crises, but an after-crisis review plan will be necessary regardless of crisis. A *post-crisis review* should be conducted immediately following the crisis. A post-crisis review includes:

- tying up loose ends with stakeholders, including outlining the crisis resolution through various media outlets used throughout the crisis;
- recognizing responders who helped during the crisis;
- reviewing the response actions, including what to change and/or improve for the future;
- revisiting media coverage to ensure messages were consistent and salient and clarify any pending items; and
- updating communication plans and the strategic plan, as necessary.

It is always important to consider the emotional distress of crisis impacted individuals and the community through a crisis and during communications with stakeholders. This includes survivors, friends, family and other loved ones of crisis impacted individuals, first responders and recovery workers, nonprofit staff and volunteers involved in crisis response or impacted by the crisis, and other community members. Communication after a crisis may include resources for these groups on coping with grief after crisis or other traumatic events, information on helping children, parents, caregivers or teachers cope, tips for disaster responders, violence resources, school shooting resources, tips on managing stress and other resources that may be relevant for each crisis. These resources can be selectively included in communications at appropriate times and on appropriate delivery means, depending on the crisis.

Strategy Development

Within all the phases of strategic planning models, an emphasis is placed on decision-making and justification. Numerous theories and studies investigate the process of decision-making. The premier scholar in this field is Herbert Simon (1979), who challenged a relatively accepted belief that every individual uses rational decision-making. The *rational decision-making theory* posits that everyone makes decisions based on logical reasons and facts. Making a rational decision would mean going through the following steps:

1. Identify the problem requiring a solution.
2. Identify a solution scenario.
3. Perform a gap analysis (i.e., determine results of each potential choice).
4. Gather facts, opinions and alternatives.
5. Analyze option outcomes.
6. Select the best possible options.

7. Implement the decision to solve the problem.
8. Evaluate the final outcome.

Although seemingly thorough, the main criticism is that individuals do not undergo an extensive research process when trying to determine a solution, and the theory does not incorporate emotions and how they affect the process. Simon (1990) soon challenged his own rational decision-making theory and generated bounded rationality theory, which posits that rationality is limited when faced with a dilemma. Humans have cognitive limitations and cannot understand every facet in its entirety. So, we make the best decision with what we know at the time with the understanding that we do not know everything. The focus is on making decisions that satisfy and are sufficient.

According to Simon (1990), the fundamental criterion guiding an individual is efficiency. The goal is to produce the largest result for the resources at hand and to make the most out of the decision. Knowing these two theoretical points, the challenge is how to translate your decision-making process into sufficient justification. Bryson (2018) refers to identifying strategic issues as the heart of any strategic planning process. The majority of strategic planning efforts surface due to challenges or crises that an organization is facing. Regardless of the cause of a crisis, the organization is usually dealing with negative effects and is invested in the strategic planning process.

Hopefully the organization has already set the stage for a crisis communication planning process by establishing an initial agreement, identifying crises the organization may face, and potential levels of impact based on these crises. In addition, they reviewed the organization's attributes and elements of a crisis communication plan. Once this is complete, it is time to formalize issues created by crises identification, definition, implementation and plans for assessment.

Strategic planning is a complex process contingent upon context. Context is the organization's internal and external environment and the environment in which is operate within. Context must be considered when choosing an approach to crisis and strategic issue identification. When it comes to strategic issue identification, there are numerous approaches that organizations can choose from to help identify, define, analyze and evaluate issues and challenges. Utilizing these challenges and adapting them to crisis communication planning, you can utilize Table 6.4 to determine which approach is most appropriate for your organization (Bryson, 2018; Coombs, 2012; Haupt & Azevedo, 2021; Lerbinger, 1997; Nutt & Backoff, 1993; Ray, 1999). The approaches include the direct approach, indirect approach, goals approach, vision of success approach, visual strategy mapping approach, alignment approach, issues-tension approach and systems analysis approach (Bryson, 2018).

To briefly elaborate on the approaches, the *direct approach* occurs when planners review mandates, mission, and conduct a SWOC/T analysis to

Table 6.4 Strategic Issue Identification for Crisis Communication Planning

Direct approach	The committee conducts a review of the organization's mandates, mission and environment and determines how the crisis *directly* impacts the organization. A committee can use this inductive approach even if they don't have agreed-upon goals or authoritative hierarchy. This approach is where a committee can, essentially, create structure from chaos.
Indirect approach	The committee conducts a review of the organization's mandates, mission, results of stakeholder and SWOT analyses, agreed-upon goals and any other relevant information. Through deductive methods, the committee will systematically review these materials and determine where strategic redirection is needed. This approach differs from the direct approach in that there are agreed-upon goals, visions of success and hierarchical authority. This approach is utilized with already generated strategies.
Goals approach	By focusing on the goals, the committee identifies reputational versus operational goals, and they develop strategies to achieve these goals. In this approach, identifying strategic issues may not be the priority since they are working toward enhancing organizational performance during a crisis. A unique aspect of this approach is how it can uncover existing consensus about goals and divergences. This approach depends on detailed definitions of organizational goals and having detailed objectives to provide guidance for strategy development when crises occur.
Vision of success approach	This approach is often seen in organizations where there is new leadership or when there is a realization that programs and services do not coincide with the vision of the organization when a crisis is occurring. This approach touches upon the idea of "If you build it they will come" and provides a holistic approach where the conception of the vision is necessary to enable organizational change.
Visual strategy mapping approach	The committee maps out potential actions the organization may take during a crisis, how they will be implemented and why they are connected. The focus is on cause-and-effect relationships. Visually mapping out these relationships allows committees to see clusters of potential actions and identify disconnects that may be strategic issues. Although mapping can result in hundreds of interconnected relationships, the visual map helps make sense of complex issues and allow for a more comprehensive understanding of those issues.

(Continued)

Table 6.4 (Continued)

Alignment approach	This approach focuses on how organizational attributes connect to governance, management, and operational policies and procedures. It takes the approach that the organization is the sum of all of its parts. There must be logical connections between every facet of the organization, and these connections must be understood and integrated into every action. If one manager or process is out of alignment, then that is where the strategic issue exists.
Issues-tension approach	This approach examines four basic tensions. The tensions connect to (1) human resources; (2) innovation and change; (3) maintenance of tradition; and (4) productivity improvement. By understanding these tensions, committees can determine the best way to frame the issue or crisis. The question is whether the cost of incorrectly framing an issue is high or if the issue is very complex making framing difficult. "Strategic planners can gain enormous influence over the strategic planning process and its outcomes if the issues are framed in such a way that decision-makers must share power in order to resolve the issues" (Bryson, 2018, p. 216).
Systems analysis approach	Framing of issues or crises for the organizational system is the main focus. This approach hinges on having technical expertise in systems analysis and, therefore, means that any organization which can pay, can play. Systems analysis is a method of studying an organization through identifying its basic elements and their relationships with the aid of mathematics or computer modeling. By viewing the organization as a system, the strategic planning committee can learn more about how the organization behaves, its feedback loops and how connected the organization's basic elements are to the issues or crises so that they can be framed appropriately.

identify strategic issues. The *goals approach* is utilized when organizations first establish goals and objectives and identify goals related to those achieving the goals and objectives. The *vision of success approach* is when an organization develops a "best" picture of the organization in the future and identifies issues that could prevent this from being achieved. The *indirect approach* is useful when planners are unsure of the exact need of the organization but acknowledge issues are impacting performance. The *visual strategy mapping approach* involves creation of word-and-arrow diagrams in which statements about potential actions the organization might take, how they might be taken, and why, are linked by arrows indicating the cause–effect or influence relationships. The *alignment approach* helps clarify where there are gaps, inconsistencies or conflicts among the various elements of an organization's governance, management and operating policies, systems and procedures. The *issues-tension approach* focuses on aspects of human resources, innovation and change, maintenance of tradition, and productivity improvements. A *systems analysis approach* is the most complicated approach as it focuses on understanding the entire organization as a complex system and intends to understand all the mechanisms within (Bryson, 2018). Each approach has a unique way to identify strategic issues for a public or nonprofit organization and can assist in generating strategies to circumvent possible negative impacts of crises.

In essence, strategic planning for crisis communication is a messy and, at times, uncomfortable process. There are no guarantees or easy answers. The organization may need to justify decisions to numerous stakeholders who each have different levels of investment in organizational success. The executive director may be the one performing much of the work with the least amount of appreciation. The best advice is to become comfortable with the uncomfortable. Realize that planning is an imperfect process and be aware that there will be many bumps along the road.

Additional Resources Available Online for Nonprofits in Disaster and Crisis Communication Planning

American Public Transportation Association Crisis Communications Plan Template: https://sustainingplaces.files.wordpress.com/2014/03/crisiscomm.pdf

Bloomberg Crisis Communication Plan Example: https://bloomerang.co/wp-content/uploads/2016/09/Crisis-Communication-Plan.pdf

Colorado Nonprofit Association Crisis Communication Template: https://sustainingplaces.files.wordpress.com/2014/03/crisiscomm.pdf

Crisis and Emergency Risk Communications training program from the Centers for Disease Control and Prevention: http://emergency.cdc.gov/cerc/

National Institute of Environmental Health Sciences Responder and Community Resilience Resources and Training materials: https://tools.niehs.nih.gov/wetp/index.cfm?id=2528

National Mining Association Media and Community Crisis Communication Planning Template: https://nma.org/wp-content/uploads/2016/08/Crisis-Communications-Template.pdf

Nonprofit Center of North East Florida Resources for Disaster and Emergency Planning: https://nonprofitctr.org/research-resources/resources-for-disaster-and-emergency-planning/

Nonprofit Technology Enterprise Network: https://www.nten.org/article/emergency-management-for-nonprofits/

Ready.gov Business Preparedness Planning: https://www.ready.gov/business and crisis communication plan: https://www.ready.gov/crisis-communications-plan

TechSoup: Nonprofit Disaster Planning and Recovery: https://www.techsoup.org/disaster-planning-and-recovery

References

Bryson, J. M. (2018). *Strategic planning for public and nonprofit organizations: A guide to strengthening and sustaining organizational achievement*. Hoboken: John Wiley & Sons.

Ciesielka, T. C. (2015). *Crisis communications for not-for-profits resource guide*.TC Public Relations. Retrieved from https://www.tcpr.net/wp-content/uploads/2015/10/TCPR-Nonprofit-Reputation-Resource-Guide.pdf.

Colorado Nonprofit Association (2014). *Crisis communication plan: nonprofit toolkit*. Crisis Communications, 440.

Coombs, W. T. (2012). *Ongoing crisis communication: Planning, managing, and responding*. Thousand Oaks: Sage Publications.

Denhardt, R. B., Denhardt, J. V., & Aristigueta, M. P. (2016). Motivation and Engagement. *Managing Human Behavior in Public and Nonprofit Organizations*, 153–174.

Haupt, B., & Azevedo, L. (2021). Crisis communication planning and nonprofit organizations. *Disaster Prevention and Management, 30*(2), 163–178.

Lenhoff-Briggs, A. (2018). *Ten steps to effective crisis management for nonprofit organizations*. Retrieved from https://www.rjweanfdn.org/wp-content/uploads/2018/02/02.22.18-Crisis-Communications-Plan-VS.-FINAL-1.pdf.

Lerbinger, O. (1997). *The crisis manager: Facing risk and responsibility*. Mahwah: Lawrence Erlbaum Associates.

New England Insurance Services (n.d). *Crisis management for private and nonprofit social and human services providers*. Retrieved from https://www.neisinc.com/social-human-services-non-profit-insurance.htm.

Norris, S. (2015). *Crisis management: how two nonprofits handled crisis- why you should be prepared*. NonProfitPro Podcast. Retrieved from https://www.nonprofitpro.com/article/crisis-management-how-two-nonprofits-handled-crisis-and-why-you-need-to-be-prepared/all/.

Nutt, P. C., & Backoff, R. W. (1993). Organizational publicness and its implications for strategic management. *Journal of Public Administration Research and Theory, 3*(2), 209–231.

Ray, S. J. (1999). *Strategic communication in crisis management: Lessons from the airline industry*. Westport: Greenwood Publishing Group.

Shannon, M. (2015). *How to create a crisis communication plan for your nonprofit*. Nonprofit MarCommunity. Retrieved from https://nonprofitmarcommunity.com/crisis-communications-plan/.

Simon, H. A. (1979). Rational decision making in business organizations. *The American Economic Review, 69*(4), 493–513.

Simon, H. A. (1990). Bounded rationality. In *Utility and probability* (pp. 15–18). London, UK: Palgrave Macmillan.

Stephens, K. K., Malone, P. C., & Bailey, C. M. (2005). Communicating with stakeholders during a crisis: Evaluating message strategies. *The Journal of Business Communication, 42*(4), 390–419.

7 Communication with Internal and External Stakeholders

Lauren Azevedo

Organizational Context

Organizational context includes the size, structure, operations, formality and culture of a nonprofit organization. Simply put, organizational context is the environment or atmosphere of the nonprofit. Context is shaped by several factors, including the mission and programming, community, current laws, citizen expectations and community need. Nonprofits may be small, medium or large, formal or informal, operate more linearly or hierarchically, or communicate more remotely or in person. Office staff, board members or volunteers may dress in business or professional attire or in more casual attire. Board members and other organizational representatives may be referred to by their professional titles or surnames or by their first name. All of these factors contribute to the organization's context.

The context of the nonprofit influences how, when and where communication within the organization happens, both for internal and external stakeholders. There may be three types of organizational "stakes", including: (1) equity, or ownership of the organization; (2) economic, or some sort of economic interest without ownership of the organization; or (3) influencer, meaning interests held by individuals with neither economic or equity stakes, including advocates, environmental or citizen groups or other agencies (Cornelissen, 2014).

Larger nonprofits with numerous stakeholders or matrix leadership structures may be more formal in nature and meetings are likely to be structured. Information shared in these organizations is likely to be in channels like planned emails and arranged meetings with detailed agendas and may include many other methods of communication with careful coordination between leaders, executives, directors. On the other hand, small nonprofits with only few to no staff may have an open-door policy. Communication is less structured and less formal and frequently happens in offices or social settings with different stakeholders.

DOI: 10.4324/9781003147480-7

As a nonprofit leader, one responsibility is to create and sustain an appropriate organizational context that fits the mission and organizational objectives. Leaders are conversational creators and set the tone for organizational communication. As an effective communicator, organizational context must be well understood to engage with internal and external stakeholders appropriately. *Internal stakeholders* are people who have a commitment to serving the organization and include the organization's board members, staff members, volunteers and donors. *External stakeholders* are those who are impacted by the work of the organization, including service recipients, community partners and community members. Both groups of stakeholders require information that is clear and meaningful, though frequency and method of delivery will vary.

Organizational Communication

Leading within a nonprofit organizational context requires effective shaping of the work environment so that efforts made within the workplace are centered on the mission, keeping sustainability in mind. Stakeholder relationships are critical for nonprofits, because without them they cannot operate. Stakeholder relations built through active, constant and transparent communication helps with engagement and involvement, in addition to overcoming organizational challenges (Freeman et al., 2017; Van Wissen & Wonneberger, 2017). *Organizational communication*, inclusive of all communication that an organization conveys, is important for stakeholder relationships. Organizational communication has four classifications, including: verbal and nonverbal communication, one-way or two-way communication, interpersonal and mass communication, and internal and external communication (Blundel & Ippolito, 2008).

Figure 7.1 includes the classification of communication types, along with their meaning. *Verbal communication* includes any written or oral communication using words, such as speeches and conversations. The effectiveness of verbal communication may vary on volume, tone, clarity and word choice (Denhardt, Denhardt, & Aristigueta, 2018). Verbal communication can be altered during delivery if the sender feels an effective message is not being sent. *Nonverbal communication* is communication without words, such as body language, tone and eye contact. *One-way communication* is linear, meaning communication travels from sender to receiver to advise, influence, or control (Denhardt, Denhardt, & Aristigueta, 2018). *Two-way communication* includes both the message from sender to receiver and feedback from the receiver back to the sender to ensure the message was received. *Interpersonal communication* happens between a small group of people, as few as two, and is more personal. Feedback happens immediately in these

Verbal vs Non-verbal	1-Way vs 2-Way	Interpersonal vs Mass	Internal vs External
• Involving words • Involving body language, tone, or eye contact	• Linear relationships between sender and received • Includes feedback after message between sender and receiver	• Involves few people on a personal level • Involves large group over mass medium	• Involves messaging inside of an organization • Involves messagin outside of an organization

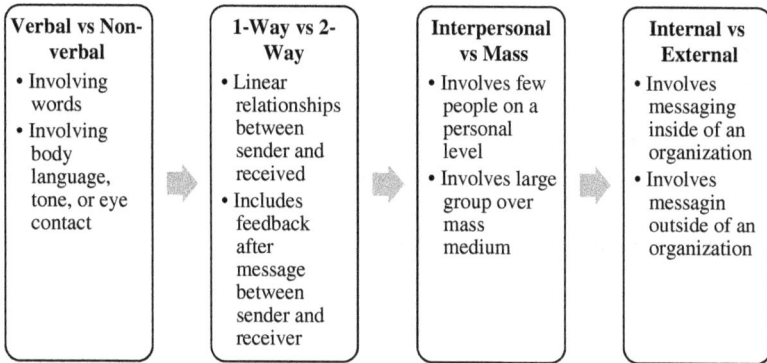

Figure 7.1 Ways to Classify Communication.

instances. *Mass communication* happens between a larger number of people and includes some sort of *mass media*, or large-scale platform to send the message to a group of people that usually utilizes a technological channel. Examples include websites, radio or news networks or social media. Finally, *internal communication* involves information sharing within an organization whereas *external communication* involves information sharing outside of an organization.

Communicating during Crises

Preparation is key in sharing information with stakeholders before, during and after crises. Leaders should be well prepared for any crisis type on what information needs to be shared, who is sharing it and who the point of contact is for questions. Conversations with internal and external stakeholders regarding crisis plans must begin during non-crisis periods to allow for discussion of any preconceived challenges. Additionally, this provides an opportunity to practice the plan and work out any potential kinks prior to activation. It is also important for leaders to act in a manner consistent with the messages they are portraying. If inconsistent actions occur, a leader may be deemed a "hypocrite" which will inevitably produce negative consequences for the organization.

Those who are responsible for talking to the media, taking questions via email or social media, and presenting information to the community should ensure that the same information is shared across platforms. Within the crisis team, a *crisis communication coordinator* or leader should be identified and can help ensure communication is accurate and streamlined.

In small nonprofits the crisis communication coordinator may be the executive director. In large organizations, the crisis communication coordinator may be a designated member of the marketing and communication team and crisis team and can work closely with the executive director during a crisis. This helps mitigate misinformation sharing and ensures messages are streamlined. Presenting false or contradictory information to stakeholders during a crisis could be detrimental for nonprofit reputation and trust.

Communicating with Stakeholders

Communicating with stakeholders is becoming increasingly dynamic, as organizations today face new challenges regarding digital technologies, blurred organizational boundaries and increased stakeholder thinking (Blundel & Ippolito, 2008), in addition to operating within controversial social, political and economic contexts. Becoming a publisher of content has never been easier in terms of access, as new technologies and the internet are abundant; however, with that access comes increased need for training on technology and on message appropriateness. The implications for nonprofits to keep up with modern technologies is important for remaining relevant and legitimate, as citizen demand for accurate, timely and transparent information has increased (Twizeyimana & Andersson, 2019). This has presented opportunities for nonprofits to leverage these resources to bring value to their communities and promote their mission.

Leaders must understand how to communicate with stakeholders effectively and meaningfully within their environment, which includes identifying specific stakeholders, understanding appropriate messaging for different groups, engaging effectively, managing their expectations and keeping track of communications (Brønn & Brønn, 2003; Dawkins, 2004). These vital parts of communicating are seen in Figure 7.2. Leaders also have a responsibility to present information to stakeholders in ways that match or reflect the professional image and organizational context (Ray, 1999). Although these communication steps can work for some crises, others require more immediate response which can inhibit organizational access to stakeholders. Even if communication is immediate, it is important to ensure messaging and responses align with the organization's mission and past action, as stakeholders may reject messaging during a crisis when those messages are not consistent with prior actions (Cowden & Sellnow, 2002). For this reason, stakeholder communication should be a clear and detailed part of the crisis communication plan.

Identifying Stakeholders

Stakeholders can be classified in many ways, such as by their donor status, their contractual relationship (such as staff, shareholders, distributors) or by

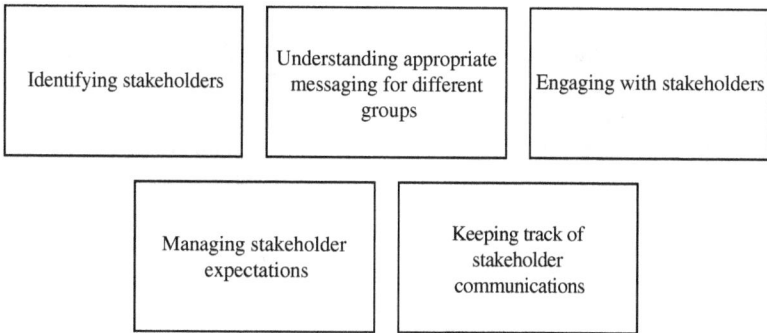

Figure 7.2 Communicating with Stakeholders.

their community affiliation (such as service recipients, government, partner agencies). Nonprofit leaders should carefully identify all stakeholder groups, in addition to any relevant subgroups. For instance, a nonprofit may have a stakeholder group of donors and divide these into major donors, corporate donors, foundations, prospects, etc. Each of these stakeholder groups should be carefully identified, including how individuals may fit into more than one stakeholder group. Keeping in mind that not all stakeholders care about the same thing, nonprofit leaders must find ways to manage conflicting interests and preferences. Thus, it is essential to develop appropriate messaging that creates value for all groups, which is often a multistep messaging approach.

Understanding Appropriate Messaging for Different Groups and Different Crises

Once all stakeholder groups are carefully identified, leaders must consider what each of these groups cares about, including their interests and priorities. This will help to determine what information is needed from organizational leadership. Every communication may not be used by every stakeholder group; yet, all stakeholder groups should receive the same message to ensure credibility and legitimacy (Coombs, 1999). Communication that is interpersonal will be more tailored to recipients; however, even communication over media platforms should be direct, relevant and provide the same information. Leaders must also realize that mistakes can be made in assuming stakeholder feelings or beliefs and only find out differently during a crisis. Sometimes, stakeholders may distance themselves from the organization or crisis because they fear guilt by association or negative media depiction, and they want to protect their own interests (Pearson & Mitroff, 1993).

Communication strategies will change for different stakeholder groups depending on the crisis type and stage. Chapter 2 covers the stages of non-profit crisis and crisis strategies. Nearly all nonprofit crises unfold in four overarching phases including warning signs of impending disaster, preparation and prevention, damage control and recovery (Pearson & Mitroff, 1993; Stephens et al, 2005). Throughout each phase of the crisis, information may vary, particularly as more becomes known in terms of crisis impact. As the organization begins to recover, for example, it may be appropriate to share more detailed information and show organizational changes or progress in a visual communication format.

Certain crisis types may require additional experts on the crisis team for communicating information to stakeholders. For instance, if a crisis involves a medical situation that impacts a large stakeholder group, there may be a need for technical translation within communication. Zehr (1999) suggests that the need for technical translation will increase with more use of technology. When crises involve highly technical or scientific ideas, communication to address these issues may include elucidating explanations, such as giving examples and nonexamples to explain the issue, quasi-scientific explanations to help receivers understand through pictures or metaphors, or transformative explanations, that help challenge receivers' beliefs (McKeachie, 1994; Rowan, 1999; Stephens et al., 2005). Ensuring that crisis communication plans include technical translations into prepared messages is important for proactive crisis response (Stephens et al., 2005).

Engaging with Stakeholders

As nonprofit leaders identify their stakeholder groups and better understand appropriate messages for each group, the method of engagement should be considered. There are many ways to engage with stakeholders. Some of the most popular ways to engage among nonprofits include annual reports, meetings, newsletters and social media (Waters, Burnett, Lamm, & Lucas, 2009). Social media can help nonprofits improve advocacy, impact donor behavior and better communicate with their stakeholders (Guo & Saxton, 2014; Hu & Shi, 2017; Lovejoy & Saxton, 2012). These and other mechanisms for stakeholder engagement are seen in Figure 7.3.

To better understand how external stakeholders want to be engaged, leaders can ask their preferred communication during standard interactions. Once there is a general understanding of how stakeholders prefer to be communicated with, the organization should provide multiple ways for stakeholders to give input. Using mediums that offer two-way communication

Annual reports	Meetings	Funder reports
Fundraising events	Press releases	Newsletter
Socialmedia	Task force participation/ networking	Public testimony (city council meetings, etc.)

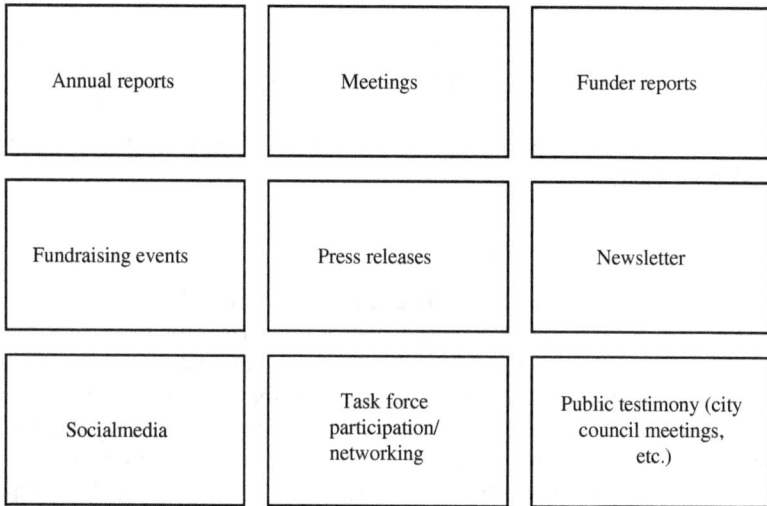

Figure 7.3 Methods of Stakeholder Engagement.

can involve stakeholders in various efforts including planning and programming, rather than simply informing through one-way communication. An appropriate amount of involvement among stakeholders can increase organizational value and improve stakeholder relationships (Van Wissen & Wonneberger, 2017).

Engagement with internal stakeholders is critical for morale and turnover, which could impact fundraising objectives, programming and mission fulfillment. To engage with internal stakeholders, leaders should build a culture of trust, invest in their employees, both financially and in non-financial means including development and training, and listen to information shared with internal stakeholders during crisis, which should be concise, meaningful, timely, relevant, clear, given in necessary context and accessible (Seppänen & Virrantaus, 2015). Depending on the crisis type and timeline, leaders should consider the appropriateness of one-way vs two-way communication for internal stakeholders.

During a crisis, communication to stakeholders should happen quickly. Two-way communication is not always the best way to get information out judiciously depending on the crisis type and stage. It is also important to leverage the organization's networks during the crisis. Leaders should also keep in mind the victims of the crisis and be considerate of their circumstances in communication. Many stakeholders can be affected during crisis and organizational response or become more involved as the crisis continues. Stakeholders may cross boundaries as they become more involved in crises (Lerbinger, 1997). It is a good practice to avoid placing blame and remain transparent in these communications. Finally, leaders must ensure consistent messaging (Eldridge, Hampton, & Marfell, 2020; Stephens et al., 2005). When leaders are well prepared, crisis communication can be a chance for leaders to demonstrate to their constituents how they are valued in the public domain.

Managing Stakeholder Expectations

Stakeholder expectations must be understood and weighed appropriately against the organization's mission and values, organizational context and the public good (Balser & McClusky, 2005). Managing relations is important for perceived *accountability* and *legitimacy* (Ospina, Diaz, & O'Sullivan, 2002). Nonprofits manage their stakeholder relations by balancing conflicting expectations and internal objectives and compromising between the two (Oliver, 1991; Alexander, 1996). Consistently grounding stakeholder relations in good nonprofit management practices, so that they are aligned with the mission, vision, values and capabilities of the nonprofit, will enhance perceived responsiveness to stakeholders (Balser & McClusky, 2005). Additionally, keeping stakeholders engaged by using some methods of two-way communication can help manage expectations and organizational objectives.

Having board members call donors can be an excellent method of interpersonal, two-way communication in non-crisis times. This may be a particularly valuable tool for thanking donors and recognizing their gifts, inviting them to events or filling them in on relevant decisions regarding their gift(s) and programming. However, this same interpersonal communication may not be feasible in crisis situations. Prompt communication with stakeholders, which includes information regarding where to go for follow up communication or organizational updates, should be shared in initial communication. This will help manage stakeholder expectations regarding frequency and platforms used for gathering information through the crisis. Keep in mind, however, that credibility is a form of currency, and therefore it is important to follow through with communication and information commitments.

Keeping Track of Stakeholder Communications

Keeping track of communication to and from stakeholders is vital to ensure timely and consistent communications, particularly during crises. Understanding how nonprofits gather and engage in information and communication will help in preparing future communications and better manage crisis response. It may be beneficial to break stakeholder groups and lists into preferred communication channels. This can assist leaders with personalizing communication and ensuring information is shared in a timely way for each group. This will also help ensure message consistency for different groups and help the organization keep communication commitments, particularly through crisis. Keeping detailed records of communications is also important for media requests and insurance purposes, in the case that the crisis involves legal action with the organization.

Summary of Key Points

- Nonprofit context influences communication in day-to-day activities and during crises. It is the leader's responsibility to create and sustain an appropriate organizational context that fits the mission and organizational objectives.
- Communicating with internal and external stakeholders is important for garnering support and managing reputation during a crisis. Organizational communication can be classified in different ways, including verbal and nonverbal communication, one-way or two-way communication, interpersonal and mass communication, and internal and external communication.
- Nonprofit leaders should ensure organizational messages align with the organization's mission and past action.
- The key to nonprofit crisis management is preparation. Leaders should be aware of their organization's crisis plans, which should include prepared messaging for any crisis type. Conversations with internal and external stakeholders regarding crisis plans must begin during non-crisis times.
- Within the crisis team, a *crisis communication coordinator* or leader should be identified and can help ensure communication is accurate and streamlined.
- Although crises create uncertain environments, nonprofits may leverage or capitalize crisis times to tell the community about their mission, values and program offerings.
- Crises can provide a way to better understand who is most important to a nonprofit organization during a certain time or context. Understanding and preparing for various crisis communication with all identified stakeholder groups can situate nonprofits recover and be better prepared in the future.

Discussion Questions

1. Why is understanding the nonprofit's organizational context important for crisis communication?
2. How is organizational communication important for stakeholder relationships?
3. In what ways can organizational communication be classified? Is one classification method more important than another during crisis times?
4. How can stakeholder communication be best managed? What mechanisms or strategies can be employed for best including these communications in the crisis communication plan?

References

Alexander, V. D. (1996). Pictures at an exhibition: Conflicting pressures in museums and the display of art. *American Journal of Sociology*, *101*(4), 797–839.

Balser, D., & McClusky, J. (2005). Managing stakeholder relationships and nonprofit organization effectiveness. *Nonprofit Management and Leadership*, *15*(3), 295–315.

Blundel, R., & Ippolito, K. (2008). *Effective organisational communication: Perspectives, principles and practices*. Richmond: Pearson Education.

Brønn, P. S., & Brønn, C. (2003). A reflective stakeholder approach: Co-orientation as a basis for communication and learning. *Journal of Communication Management*, *7*(4), 291–303.

Coombs, W. T. (1999). Information and compassion in crisis responses: A test of their effects. *Journal of Public Relations Research*, *11*(2), 125–142.

Cornelissen, J. 2014. *Corporate communication. A guide to theory & practice.* 4th ed. London, UK: Sage Publications.

Cowden, K., & Sellnow, T. L. (2002). Issues advertising as crisis communication: Northwest Airlines' use of image restoration strategies during the 1998 pilot's strike. *The Journal of Business Communication*, *39*(2), 193–219.

Dawkins, J. (2004). Corporate responsibility: The communication challenge. *Journal of Communication Management*, *9*(2), 108–119.

Denhardt, R. B., Denhardt, J. V., Aristigueta, M. P., & Rawlings, K. C. (2018). *Managing human behavior in public and nonprofit organizations*. Washington: CQ Press.

Eldridge, C. C., Hampton, D., & Marfell, J. (2020). Communication during crisis. *Nursing Management*, *51*(8), 50–53.

Freeman, R. E., Kujala, J., Sachs, S., & Stutz, C. (2017). Stakeholder engagement: Practicing the ideas of stakeholder theory. In *Stakeholder engagement: Clinical Research Cases* (pp. 1–12). Berlin, Germany: Springer.

Guo, C., & Saxton, G. D. (2014). Tweeting social change: How social media are changing nonprofit advocacy. *Nonprofit and Voluntary Sector Quarterly*, *43*(1), 57–79.

Hu, Q., & Shi, W. (2017). Understanding nonprofit organizations' use of social networking sites: An examination of management factors. *International Journal of Public Administration in the Digital Age (IJPADA), 4*(1), 19–34.

Lerbinger, O. (1997). The crisis manager: Facing risk and responsibility (book review). *Journalism and Mass Communication Quarterly, 74*(3), 646.

Lovejoy, K., & Saxton, G. D. (2012). Information, community, and action: How nonprofit organizations use social media. *Journal of Computer-Mediated Communication, 17*(3), 337–353.

McKeachie, W. J. (1994). *Teaching tips: Strategies, research, and theory for college and university teachers.* Lexington: DC Heath & Co.

Oliver, C. (1991). Strategic responses to institutional processes. *Academy of Management Review, 16*(1), 145–179.

Ospina, S., Diaz, W., & O'sullivan, J. F. (2002). Negotiating accountability: Managerial lessons from identity-based nonprofit organizations. *Nonprofit and Voluntary Sector Quarterly, 31*(1), 5–31.

Pearson, C. M., & Mitroff, I. I. (1993). From crisis prone to crisis prepared: A framework for crisis management. *Academy of Management Perspectives, 7*(1), 48–59.

Ray, S. J. (1999). *Strategic communication in crisis management lessons from the airline industry.* Westport: Quorum.

Rowan, K. E. (1999). Effective explanation of uncertain and complex science. In S. M. Friedman, S. Dunwoody & C. L. Rogers (Eds.), *Communicating uncertainty: Media coverage of new and controversial science* (pp. 210–224). England, UK: Routledge.

Seppänen, H., & Virrantaus, K. (2015). Shared situational awareness and information quality in disaster management. *Safety Science, 77,* 112–122.

Stephens, K. K., Malone, P. C., & Bailey, C. M. (2005). Communicating with stakeholders during a crisis: Evaluating message strategies. *The Journal of Business Communication, 42*(4), 390–419.

Twizeyimana, J. D., & Andersson, A. (2019). The public value of E-Government – A literature review. *Government Information Quarterly, 36*(2), 167–178. https://doi.org/10.1016/j.giq.2019.01.001

Van Wissen, N., & Wonneberger, A. (2017). Building stakeholder relations online: How nonprofit organizations use dialogic and relational maintenance strategies on Facebook. *Communication Management Review, 2*(01), 54–74.

Waters, R. D., Burnett, E., Lamm, A., & Lucas, J. (2009). Engaging stakeholders through social networking: How nonprofit organizations are using Facebook. *Public Relations Review, 35*(2), 102–106.

Zehr, S. C. (1999). Scientists representations of uncertainty. In S. M. Friedman, S. Dunwoody, & C. L. Rogers (Eds.), *Communicating uncertainty: Media coverage of new and controversial science* (pp. 3–21). England, UK: Routledge.

8 Implementing the Crisis Communication Plan

Brittany "Brie" Haupt

Introduction

A potential positive impact occurs when implementing strategies and entering into the management portion of strategic planning. Putting strategies into action hinges on the inclusion of individuals who may not be a part of the planning committee. Remember, a key component of implementation is effective management. For management to be effective, plans must be thoroughly detailed, managers must understand the organizational vision and there needs to be an evaluation process. To assist with the implementation process, the crisis communication planning committee should incorporate a three-phase approach: information-seeking, instructing and adjusting. In addition, there are general guidelines to implementation along with communication and educational guidelines and personnel recommendations. The planning committee should also consider a direct or stage implementation to the crisis communication plan. Yet, the committee should encourage the responsible entities to practice the crisis communication plan during non-crisis periods and in a simulated environment.

The Implementation Process

The *implementation process* can be broken down into three phases: information-seeking, instructing and adjusting. The *information-seeking phase* is breaking down the crisis communication plan into logistical components where the organization identifies how the strategies will be laid out in the organization. The organization also must identify who needs to be responsible for what components, what resources need to be shifted, timelines for completion, etc.

The *instructing phase* is where the organization brings responsible entities together and makes sure they understand their role in the implementation process and what *feedback loops* exist. For example, if the organization

DOI: 10.4324/9781003147480-8

is engaging in changing the after-school program and is changing the date, time, food and shuttle services, then the organization must make sure that the person in charge of actually conducting the program is aware of these new changes and how it alters their current pattern of operation. That person also needs to know who to talk to if the shuttle is late or the food is not delivered or if there are any issues that surface. These processes are considered feedback loops.

The next phase is the *adjusting phase*. The organization engages in a trial period of sorts to see how it goes and to see what adjustments need to be made. This is where idealism meets reality. Ideally, the organization can envision the after-school program going off without a hitch, but, in reality, the organization will have students and parents who mix up days, food that is not delivered or does not adhere to allergy requests, shuttles that are delayed, or the realization that the organization needs additional resources and individuals, etc. The organization enters this adjustment period and makes the necessary changes, and then the organization lets the program continue until an agreed-upon date where the evaluation and assessment process begins.

The next part of the process is preparing a *crisis communication center* location for the crisis communication plan, like an emergency operations center (EOC). This location is where crisis managers direct all the emergency support functions and gather all essential personnel. The crisis headquarters is the nonprofit's EOC and place where the crisis is managed. Along with establishing a headquarters, the organization can create a crisis response kit that includes essential items, such as written crisis communication plans, notebooks, pencils, pens, computers, necessary chargers, backup generators, emergency services telephone numbers, list of staff and volunteers, emergency contact numbers, support services, and numbers, media contacts, flashlights, weather radio, blankets, first aid kits, bottled water, snacks and other necessities (NEIS, n.d.). The headquarters is also a place to have any relevant files organized and have the ability to prepare reports for distribution. It is important to note that the crisis communication center may not be needed if dealing with crises that are internal to the organization.

Implementation Guidelines

When it comes to implementation, there are several guidelines organizations may find useful and can be broken down into general guidelines, communication, and educational considerations, personnel tips and direct versus staged implementation (Bryson, 2018; Haupt, 2021).

General Guidelines

For general guidelines, nonprofit organizations should consciously and deliberately plan and manage implementation in a strategic way. This incorporates leaders thinking and anticipating stakeholder concerns and incorporating them into the crisis communication plan. In addition, there must be an organized, systemic plan to implement the crisis communication plan (Bryson, 2018). The implementation strategy is a part of the crisis communication plan and focuses attention on the necessary decisions, actions and responsible parties. It assists with being able to manage the crisis communication plan and the responsibilities of the included entities (Bryson, 2018; Haupt, 2021).

It is critical to remember that the crisis communication plan is a document focused on how to implement strategies for short-term and long-term goals. It usually consists of:

- specific expected results, objectives and milestones;
- roles and responsibilities of involved organizations and individuals;
- specific crisis strategies based on crisis types;
- resource and support requirements and sources;
- communication feedback process;
- review and monitoring process; and,
- accountability processes and procedures.

Additional general guidelines include focusing on changes that can be introduced easily and rapidly. Make sure the changes are conceptually clear and incorporate evidence of cause-effect relationships. Verify that there is buy-in for the crisis communication plan from both internal and external stakeholders of the organization. Moreover, try to reduce the number of administrative tasks and include a testing period, if possible, to try out the changes before changes are implemented throughout the organization. The organization should also incorporate incentives or benefits for involved entities if they have the resources to do so (Bryson, 2018; Haupt, 2021).

Focusing on each strategy, the organization should break down the crisis communication strategies into smaller pieces and build in enough people, time, attention, money, administrative and support services and other resources to ensure successful implementation, such as technical assistance, monies for unforeseen circumstances, training and professional development funds. This is more easily accomplished when linked to ongoing operations and maintained by a coalition of implementers, advocates and interest groups intent on effective implementation of the crisis communication plan and willing to protect the organization (Bryson, 2018; Haupt, 2021). In terms of policies, organizational, legislative, executive and administrative policies and actions should facilitate rather than impede implementation. This is done through the creation of *green tape*, or rules that facilitate effective implementation, and reduction of red tape, which adds administrative steps to implementation.

Conflict resolution is another area to consider when it comes to general implementation guidelines. Every change, even minor ones, will impact organizational culture. The more attention given to educating organizational members about the changes and supporting buy-in mitigates potential conflict. Focusing on management, the organization should create an accountability system that assures key stakeholders that political, legal and performance-based accountability needs are met. This is done by focusing on a balance between top-down direction and bottom-up efforts and learning; moreover, utilizing performance information in decision-making and promoting strong leaders and commitment. Lastly, it is imperative to remember that implementation takes time and requires attention, resources and effort (Haupt, 2021).

Communication and Educational Guidelines

For communication and educational components, the organization should invest in *capacity building* communication activities. Capacity building includes any activity that can improve the ability of a nonprofit to achieve its mission and remain sustainable. It is fundamentally an improvement in organizational or network effectiveness and can include activities that make the organization and its programs stronger, such as creating strategic plans and crisis communication plans. Members of the organization should hear about the proposed changes through multiple channels to increase the chance for messages to sink in and be allowed to talk about the proposed changes to help them process what needs to be done (Bryson, 2018). Emphasizing learning generates a culture of receptiveness to change. Learning forums are a way to educate organizational members along with tailored training and professional development. The organization can also utilize formative and development evaluations to facilitate adaptive learning. An additional way to educate organizational members about the changes is through strategic marketing. Select information and communication technologies and social media outlets that can help support implementation and ongoing learning efforts. The organization should also work to reduce resistance based on divergent attitudes and lack of participation. Strategically utilize orientation sessions, training materials, problem-solving sessions, one-on-one training and technical assistance to get everyone on the same page (Bryson, 2018; Haupt, 2021).

Personnel Guidelines

Ultimately, the implementation process relies on the people involved. Set it up for success wherever possible! This begins with hiring or staffing the most qualified individuals with crisis communication skills and background experience. Personnel also appreciate adequate compensation, career advancement opportunities and professional development. Moreover, the organization should consider developing a guiding vision of success if one has not been developed already. There also needs to be regular assessment periods that align with the timeline for implementing the crisis communication plan and incorporate the specific responsibilities of involved entities. A way to ensure this integration is by giving the planning committee the task of managing implementation or establishing a new implementation team with significant overlap in membership with the planning team. Additional support is given when personnel have access to, and can liaison with, leaders during implementation (Bryson, 2018; Haupt, 2021).

It is critical the organization anticipates personnel conflicts. Give special attention to how the organization will reorganize personnel or transition them out of current roles. Try not to work around or avoid personnel who are not likely to help the change effort. It is a difficult process, but success hinges on the people. Perhaps create a new department or unit rather than give responsibilities to existing entities deemed antagonistic to the process. Reorganize, if necessary, but make sure the moves result in increased morale and productivity. Lastly, create policies to reward organizational members who actively support the implementation strategies (Bryson, 2018; Haupt, 2021).

Direct and Staged Implementation Process

An additional area of consideration is the timeline for implementation. Consider a direct or staged implementation process for any crisis communication strategies in tandem with whether the organization is experiencing a crisis or is in a non-crisis period (Bryson, 2018; Haupt, 2021). *Direct implementation* is best when the situation is technically, and politically, simple and immediate action is necessary for system survival in a crisis. Changes occur immediately without testing or phased implementation. Conversely, consider staged implementation in difficult situations. *Staged implementation* presumes that implementation will occur in stages or waves. The organization can either begin with the first stage of implementers and then follow with stages or waves until all strategies are in action, or systematically incorporate implementation strategies with as many organizational members as possible and then stage or wave out the remaining strategies. Testing usually incorporates prototypes or demonstrations whenever possible.

Parallel to the implementation process selected, the organization should design crisis communication training and exercises to support the effectiveness. These training and exercises can test whether the proposed changes produce the desired effects and should be performed in a safe and controlled environment with access to resources. The findings of these training and exercises could result in some plan changes that must be communicated to internal and external stakeholders. Should this occur then the organization needs substantial resources for communication tactics and focus on educational materials and operational guides, technical assistance, problem-solving, incentives for adopting changes, and flexibility. Lastly, when the implementation process is staged, give special attention to those who will implement changes in the early stages so they are supported in the process.

Before Implementation: Practice!

Prior to implementing any crisis communication plan, it would benefit the organization to perform a table top or simulation exercise. These types of exercises allow the organization to practice a crisis communication plan before implementation. The purpose of exercising the crisis communication plan during a non-crisis period is to determine any issues that may surface in terms of procedures, communication message issues, stakeholder impact, etc.

The Federal Emergency Management Agency (FEMA, 2022) defines tabletop exercises as "an instrument to train for, assess, practice, and improve performance in prevention, protection, response, and recovery capabilities in a risk-free environment". FEMA regularly utilizes table top exercises to test and validate policies, plans, procedures, equipment and more. These exercises also allow participating organizations the ability to clarify roles and responsibilities and improve coordination and communication. Participants of tabletop exercises usually consist of key personnel with emergency or crisis management roles and responsibilities that would be needed during a specific crisis event. Since the exercise is conducted in a non-crisis time period and in a simulated environment, the participants can engage in a calm way and troubleshoot issues that surface. These exercises can occur over the course of a few hours to a few days depending on the number of participants, the crisis plan being rehearsed and resources available.

The scale of the exercise can also vary from a general walkthrough to a full-scale simulation. A *walkthrough* is useful for very basic training and is focused on familiarizing participants with their roles and responsibilities. It is less time-consuming and can provide a space for everyone to get on the same page. A *tabletop exercise* incorporates more coordinated discussions among participants to discuss the crisis communication plan and engage the participants in how they would react. A facilitator is helpful in this process and can provide additional information or nuances to the exercises to add more depth and complexity. A *functional exercise* takes the tabletop exercise into a simulated crisis environment where a scenario is given and the organization must make decisions as if the crisis were occurring. The added stress and urgency of the simulation allows for participants to practice different procedures and plan elements to see what the impact could be. A *full-scale exercise* is the most in-depth and real experience for participants. The full-scale exercise incorporates representatives from all stakeholders and community partners. This exercise is not just for internal participants but external participants and allows feedback from external entities.

In addition to the variety of exercises, there is a variety of participants:

- *Participant* – individuals willing to engage to the fullest of their ability with the mindset that the exercise is meant to identify potential issues and solve problems along with highlighting successes of the exercise.
- *Facilitator* – an individual who controls the flow of the exercise and keeps time. This individual also encourages discussion and focuses on identifying issues and the solutions presentence.
- *Evaluator* – this individual documents the outcomes of the exercise – positive and negative. They also provide feedback on recommendations and needs for future planning and training.
- *Observer* – this individual is responsible for passively following the exercise and providing additional feedback that may not be caught by the participants, facilitator or evaluator.

As with any activity, there are pros and cons to these types of practice events.

Tabletop exercises are relatively low-cost and yet highly effective in evaluating a plan and determining implementation issues. Additionally, the low-stress environment of many tabletop exercises allows participants to calmly work out issues, clarify roles and responsibilities and identify best practices.

Another benefit of tabletops is they can be conducted virtually if needed. The cons of these exercises are they cannot fully simulate an actual crisis or cause the type of real-world anxiety that a crisis situation invokes. In addition, the exercises will not strain organizational resources or participant abilities like a crisis situation will.

Summary of Key Points

- The information-seeking phase is breaking down the crisis communication plan into logistical components where the organization identifies how the strategies will be laid out in the organization.
- The instructing phase is where the organization brings responsible entities together and makes sure they understand their role in the implementation process and what feedback loops exist.
- The adjusting phase is when the organization engages in a trial period of sorts to see how it goes and to see what adjustments need to be made. This is where idealism meets reality.
- The crisis communication center location is where crisis managers direct all the emergency support functions and gather all essential personnel; the crisis headquarters is the nonprofit's emergency operations center and place where the crisis is managed.
- Depending on the timeline and context, a direct or staged implementation process needs to be considered.
- Practice! Practicing the plan is essential to implementation as it allows the low-stress environment of many tabletop exercises, allows participants to calmly work out issues, clarify roles and responsibilities and identify best practices,

Discussion Questions

1. What are the phases of implementation?
2. What is a crisis communication center?
3. What are some general guidelines?
4. What are communication and educational components?
5. What personnel considerations are recommended?
6. How do direct and staged implementations differ?

References

Bryson, J. M. (2018). *Strategic planning for public and nonprofit organizations: A guide to strengthening and sustaining organizational achievement*. Hoboken: John Wiley & Sons.

Federal Emergency Management Agency. (2022). *Exercises*. Retrieved from https://www.fema.gov/emergency-managers/national-preparedness/exercises.

Haupt, B. (2021). *Government, industry, and strategic planning: Course notes and documents (canvas course)*. Richmond: Virginia Commonwealth University.

9 Evaluation and Assessment Strategies

Brittany "Brie" Haupt and Lauren Azevedo

Introduction

When discussing evaluation, there are a few general areas of pressure that can affect the strategic planning process: compliance, funding, staffing and time. A nonprofit may need to follow specific laws that restrict its planning efforts or perhaps its funding streams are limited. Planning is also difficult if there is not enough staff to complete the process or if there is a time constriction. When evaluating compliance, the organization is seeking to make sure specific goals with projected outcomes are completed. If these are not achieved, then there can be negative consequences, such as the following:

- Loss of grant funding
- Loss of donor base
- Lawsuits
- Removal of stakeholder support (non-monetary)
- Negative public image
- Staff leaving the organization
- Volunteers leaving the organization
- Organizational restructuring
- Mission drift

Although these negative consequences may not occur for one-time issues of achieving goals and outcomes, there is no harm in understanding the potential for negative blowback and taking each step of the strategic planning process with intention.

With funding being linked to compliance issues, an acknowledgment is needed that many public and nonprofit organizations or public programs are created solely for the purpose of achieving funding-related goals and outcomes. For many nonprofit organizations, government funding is a critical revenue stream that practitioners cannot afford to be without. The goal

DOI: 10.4324/9781003147480-9

with this external pressure is to produce outcomes without compromising the quality of the service or program.

When it comes to the evaluative portion of strategic planning, a debate exists on when this process will occur. Best practice is to incorporate evaluation methods during the goal-setting portion of strategic planning. By identifying organizational attributes, you are better able to understand context. Having a goal that you cannot evaluate within the necessary context by the end of the process is useless. Professionally, I have been a part of numerous strategic planning efforts where goals were too abstract, and individuals only realized how difficult the goal was to achieve when asked how to measure and evaluate the progress.

Overview of Evaluation in Nonprofit Organizations

In the nonprofit sector, evaluations are typically conducted to measure program outcomes or impact. Credible nonprofit evaluations include a valid design, a tool for planning, documentation of success, involvement of stakeholders and outside evaluators, contain recommendations and consider organization reputation (Fine, Thayer, & Coghlan, 2000). Evaluation within the sector is often conducted as a result of grant stipulations for programs, board or leadership requirement, or stakeholder request, but they can also be useful for evaluating internal organizational plans and policies.

Formative evaluations measure the process and implementation of program activities or organizational processes, plans and initiatives. These evaluations can be useful in documenting outputs, such as the number of crisis communication trainings or number of participants in these trainings. Summative evaluations are used to document the impact that a program, plan or policy has had throughout the lives of participants. In program evaluation, the most common summative evaluation tools often include pre-post instruments, follow-up interviews or surveys.

Stakeholder involvement is important in the evaluation process. Stakeholders can increase the likelihood of actual programmatic change based on the findings from the evaluation (Fine, Thayer, & Coghlan, 2000). Stakeholders should be invited into the evaluation process to communicate needs, elicit feedback on tools and provide recommendations to obtain or facilitate data collection methods. Stakeholders can help to understand challenges and opportunities, as well as priorities that the organization faces. Stakeholder participation ensures that their input is reflected throughout program and communication plans.

A theory of change is an excellent evaluative tool for stakeholder involvement. A theory of change identifies anticipated goals, outputs and outcomes and provides a visual description of how and in what conditions the goal will be achieved. Anticipated outputs and outcomes are not only important for program success, but they are also important communication and networking tools that can be used to support research stakeholders may use in promoting the organization.

Logic models are other tools that can link program resources with activities, outputs and short, intermediate and long-term outcomes and can help in telling program performance stories (McLaughlin & Jordan, 1999). Logic models include benefits of building a common understanding of expectations for resources, reach and improvement, helping in design or improvement, communicating program place in the organization and considering performance measurement points and evaluative issues.

Balanced scorecards are another useful evaluative and planning tool that can be used in nonprofits to balance different programs and initiatives within an organization and to consider the alignment of resources and initiatives to strategic targets (Kaplan & Norton, 1992; Martello, Watson, & Fisher, 2008). Balanced scorecards look at the interrelationships in different perspectives, including the financial perspective, customer perspective, internal business process perspective and learning and growth perspective. Balancing these various perspectives of a program or initiative can help create short-term operations that link with long-term strategy.

Reassessing and Revising Strategic Plans

Remember, planning never ends. If done well, it is a continuous process. By assessing the communication plans and the whole strategic planning process, nonprofits can be more effective for future plans and processes. Reassessment of the strategies and planning process highlights how your organization – the individuals and the entity as a whole – adapts to change. Knowing this will allow the organization to target strategies for organizational operations. Unfortunately, many organizations never give enough attention to this step.

The *reassessment process* is a review of what has been implemented to determine if they should be maintained, adapted or discontinued. The truth is the context of the organization is always changing. If there is a need to adapt or discontinue a strategy, then it is usually connected to the changing environment and context (see Figure 9.1).

Internal to the organization, assessment and evaluation can focus on resources, present processes, performance, organizational attributes, decision-making and stakeholders. Assessing and evaluating resources focuses on understanding all the resources available for organizations to implement and support programs and services. Acknowledging changes in resources can provide an easy way to identify implementation issues and what needs

Internal Factors

Resources	Present Processes	Performance	Organizational Attributes	Decision-making	Stakeholders

External Factors

Political	Economic	Social	Technological	Environmental	Legal

Figure 9.1 External and Internal Environmental Factors.

to be revised in future plans. Present processes refer to the organizational activities and tasks needed to implement and manage programs and services. If there were issues during implementation of a crisis communication plan, then there may be a need to change present processes of the organization to support more effective and timely responses. Performance focuses on the actual output of the organization as measured against its intended objectives or goals. Discrepancies between the projected objectives and the ultimate outcomes can provide space for organizations to determine what needs to occur in future events. Some questions to reflect on include: Were there issues related to individual performance or organizational performance? Was the crisis resolved in a positive or negative manner? Was the impact what the organization intended?

As discussed in Chapter 5, understanding organizational attributes and determining any impacts to those attributes by a crisis is another opportunity for assessment and evaluation. Did the organization reflect their mission and vision in their actions? Were there any mandate violations or new mandates that surfaced during the crisis? Were stakeholders, both internal and external, communicated with during the crisis in appropriate manners? Transitioning to decision-making, this refers to making choices among alternative courses of action, which may also include inaction. For this segment of assessment and evaluation, the plan can be reviewed to determine if all steps were conducted. What additional decisions needed to be made? Did the organization utilize any denial, diminish, rebuild or bolstering strategies (discussed in Chapter 3)? Did the organization understand the attribution given and the responsibility to the community? Did the organization utilize crisis specific communication strategies? The last internal area to assess and evaluate is stakeholders. Was the crisis communication plan effective in terms of stakeholder communication and engagement? Were there any stakeholders that were missed or surfaced due to the crisis? Does the organization need to conduct another stakeholder analysis or generate more specific communication templates for their stakeholders?

The changing external environment relates to political, economic, social and legal arenas. In terms of political qualities, nonprofits have diverse members from the community who volunteer as board members. Members make collective decisions and have fiduciary responsibilities in the organization's affairs. The economic context relates to funding sources for nonprofits like fees, donations, grants (government and private) and subsidies. The social environment consists of how nonprofit organizations provide services, goods and resources to meet community needs. They assist other businesses in the community to drive economic development. They fill the gap generated by public and private organizations. Legal context focuses on how the nonprofit is accountable to its board members, funders and constituents and must, therefore, uphold the legal regulations of the geographic locality it operates within.

Anticipating changes in this environment gives a starting point to the assessment process. If there have been changes in the political, economic, social and legal environment, then you can anticipate changes to the crisis communication plan in terms of roles and responsibilities, resources, internal and external stakeholders and more (Bryson, 2018).

Reassessing and Revising the Crisis Communication Plan

Just like reassessment of the strategic planning process, reassessing the crisis communication plan should happen regularly. As soon as the crisis occurs, evaluation of organizational response should be conducted. Feedback from key stakeholders and media coverage can help organizations uncover problems in the current crisis communication plan that can be changed for the next planning cycle.

The crisis communication planning worksheet, found in Appendix A, is a culmination of crisis communication strategies and promoted practices for nonprofit organizations. The worksheet is divided into pre-crisis, crisis and post-crisis sections. The pre-crisis section provides a space for the planning committee identifies the planning committee members, purpose of the committee, roles and responsibilities of committee members, organizational attributes, identification of personnel who will utilize the plan, dedicated organizational resources, internal and external communication expectations, stakeholders and stakeholder analysis results, meeting times/dates/locations and a space to acknowledge additional documentation. The additional documentation can include the initial agreement with relevant notes, emergency alert messages, decision tree matrix, phone tree, contact information, key messages and scripts, media releases, training and exercise materials, affirmation of leadership support, safety protocols and the general crisis communication plan.

Utilizing the pre-crisis portion of the worksheet as conversation points for assessment and evaluation can lead to questions such as:

- Would the crisis communication planning committee members be appropriate to update the plan based on results from implementation?
- Was the purpose of the committee understood and carried out?
- Were the roles and responsibilities adequate for planning efforts?
- Has there been an impact on the attributes of the organization? If so, how should the crisis communication plan be adapted?

- Did implementation of the crisis communication plan uncover entities needed for the future?
- Were the organizational resources identified adequate for implementation?
- Were communication expectations met for internal and external policies and procedures?
- Were the stakeholders adequately addressed? Were any stakeholders missed or not needed during implementation?
- Were the supplemental documents utilized? If so, are there any adjustments needed for future events?

The crisis period section provides a space for the committee to acknowledge initial steps that have been taken, such as alerting the crisis team, phone tree initiation, internal emergency alert dissemination and designation of a spokesperson. After the initial steps, space is given for the planning committee to identify the type of crisis that will be the focus on the plan. Once the crisis type is identified, then the committee will determine the spokesperson and official position for the nonprofit organization along with the main goals for crisis response. The next aspect is the best- and worst-case scenarios along with crisis specific strategies the organization will implement. Organizational resources for response efforts must also be identified along with the communication and notification channels, such as internal messaging systems, social media, mass media, etc. Guidelines will be needed for internal and external communications along with how the crisis could impact the organization. Ways to mitigate the impact must also be considered along with any crisis specific policies and procedures necessary for implementation. Lastly, assessment and accountability measures along with a conflict resolution process must be generated.

Utilizing the crisis portion of the worksheet as conversation points for assessment and evaluation can lead to questions such as:

- Were the initial steps of the crisis communication plan enacted? Are there any adjustments to be made to the initial steps?
- Are there any adjustments needed for the crisis type utilizing the plan? Does it need to be more specific or broad?
- Was the spokesperson effective in their role?
- Was the official position for the organization appropriate to the crisis and comprehensive?
- Were the crisis response goals met? Are there any additions needed?
- Did the best- and worst-case scenarios assist in the planning efforts?
- What were the results of the crisis communication strategies? What adjustments need to be made?

- Were the resources of the organization adequate for response efforts?
- Were the communication and notification channels adequate for the crisis? Are there any channels to add or remove?
- Were the guidelines for internal and external guidelines followed during the crisis? Are there any adaptations to be made?
- What were the anticipated impacts? How do they compare to the actual impacts of the crisis?
- Were the circumvention strategies utilized? If so, are there any to add or remove?
- Were the assessment and accountability strategies utilized? What were the results?
- Were the conflict resolutions needed? If so, what were the results?

The final section of the crisis communication planning worksheet is the post-crisis period. This is where most of the assessment and evaluation takes place. The assumption is that the plan was created prior to a crisis period and can easily be accessed once a crisis occurs. The crisis team then utilizes the insights and information from the planning committee to respond to the crisis. Once the crisis has been managed then the planning committee and crisis team will evaluate how it went. Beginning with an *after-action report* summarizing the incident, the committee and crisis team will review the strategies utilized and analyze their effectiveness.

Utilizing the post-crisis portion of the worksheet, overall questions to consider once the after-action report has been reviewed include:

- What changes need to be made?
- What learning opportunities surfaced?
- Which crisis communication strategies proved most effective? Least effective?
- What went well regarding internal and external communication strategies?
- What portion(s) of the crisis communication plan needs to be adjusted for a future crisis?
- Were there any unanticipated barriers?
- What circumvention strategies need to be added?
- What are the goals for the assessment and evaluation committee for updating the crisis communication plan?

The crisis team will also have space, in the post-crisis section, to provide preliminary assessment and evaluation results as the crisis unfolds. During a crisis, the team may not have time to have an in-depth conversation of what is going well and what they can adapt for future crises. Therefore, having a space to jot down initial observations can assist future conversations where the planning committee and crisis team breaks down the crisis response in more detail. This conversation will also include how the crisis impacted organizational policies and procedures. Were there administrative barriers that surfaced? Is there a policy or procedure that needs to be created due to the impact?

An additional area that assists in assessment and evaluation is the results of crisis communication planning exercises (referred to in Chapter 8). The range of tabletop exercises available to organizations allows for assessment and evaluation to occur prior to a crisis and can circumvent potential issues before needing to enact the plan in a crisis setting.

Leadership Roles in Making Plans Work

When it comes to planning and implementation, a variety of technical and people skills are needed for crisis communication plans to be effective and competent. These skills allow for another area of assessment and evaluation. Individuals identified to be part of the crisis communication planning committee, crisis team and those connected to implementation are given an opportunity to assess and evaluate their managerial styles, the ability to be a part of a team, and their formal and informal leadership connections. The *formal leadership* impacts how individuals connect to the organization's hierarchy and any specific roles and responsibilities they will have. The *informal leadership* impact consists of the relationships built that exist outside of the organizational hierarchy and organically involve the work and personality of its personnel.

> Crisis communication planning is not a substitute for effective leadership, but it hinges on it. Planning is simply a set of concepts, procedures and tools to help nonprofit leaders act and learn strategically on behalf of their organizations and their stakeholders.

The overarching goal is to encourage positive change and garner support when a crisis occurs and positively impact the growth and development of nonprofit organizations.

Summary of Key Points

- Two areas of pressure can affect the strategic planning process: compliance and funding.
- Federal funding is a critical revenue stream that practitioners cannot afford to be without.

- Reassessment of the strategies and planning process highlights how your organization – the individuals and the entity as a whole – adapts to change.
- Crisis communication planning is not a substitute for effective leadership. It is simply a set of concepts, procedures and tools to help planners act and learn strategically on behalf of their organizations and their stakeholders.

Discussion Questions

1. How does compliance and funding affect crisis communication?
2. What does the reassessment process allow organizations to do?
3. How does leadership affect crisis communication plans?

References

Bryson, J. M. (2018). *Strategic planning for public and nonprofit organizations: A guide to strengthening and sustaining organizational achievement*. Hoboken: John Wiley & Sons.

Fine, A. H., Thayer, C. E., & Coghlan, A. (2000). Program evaluation practice in the nonprofit sector. *Nonprofit Management and Leadership, 10*(3), 331–339.

Kaplan, R. S., & Norton, D. P. (1992). The balance scorecard-measures that drive performance. *Harvard Business Review, 70*(1), 71–79.

Martello, M., Watson, J., & Fisher, M. (2008). Implementing a balanced scorecard in a non-for-profit organization. *Journal of Business & Economics Research, 6*(9), 67–80.

McLaughlin, J. A., & Jordan, G. B. (1999). Logic models: A tool for telling your programs performance story. *Evaluation and Program Planning, 22*(1), 65–72.

10 Looking Back and Moving Forward

Adapting the Crisis Communication Plan

Lauren Azevedo

Nonprofits serve a vital role in providing services to the marginalized and most vulnerable in our communities and are often a part of emergency management services and response. The current social, political and economic climate in the United States and beyond has made organizational communication a salient issue for nonprofit reputation and resilience. The COVID-19 pandemic brought crisis planning to the forefront for many nonprofit organizations who are realizing their crisis communication plans are insufficient at best or nonexistent at worst. This text provided key strategies and resources for nonprofit organizations who are creating or revisiting their planning strategies and concerned with maintaining their operations and stakeholder support when a crisis happens.

This text showcased the importance of planning before a crisis happens starting with preparing for a potential crisis. As nonprofits, this effort starts with understanding and remaining true to the organization's mission, vision and values and setting up efficient governance and leadership structures that have the capacity to strategize and plan for crises. Nonprofit leaders can leverage crisis situations and the current environment to create new types of philanthropy, increase their visibility, create new forms of participation, address program and community equity, develop or expand their networks, increase civic engagement and improve communications with stakeholders. Although crisis inevitably presents uncertainty for nonprofits, capitalizing on their strengths can improve their roles as advocates, partners and community leaders.

Communication is an intentional activity and understanding the evolution of crisis communication helps nonprofits appropriately respond to events and learn from opportunities within the chaos. Crises can be categorized into community crisis or organizational crisis and crisis involving social constructs or technical issues. Understanding the crisis type helps nonprofits communicate with stakeholders accordingly. Situational crisis

DOI: 10.4324/9781003147480-10

communication theory is an excellent tool for leaders to assist with matching response strategies to various crisis situations and allows for contextual differences based on nonprofit need, mission and goals.

The governance structure of nonprofits can also equip nonprofits to be better prepared for crisis situations. Governance structures vary greatly and depend on organizational attributes and context. Board and executive responsibilities and relationships can be understood through several theories, such as agency theory, stakeholder theory, resource dependency theory and managerial hegemony. These can provide insight into how leaders understand, plan and develop organizational policies that respond to crises. The initial agreement among the crisis team and planning committee guides the planning process and provides a stronger foundation for when crises occur.

Strategic issue identification for crisis communication planning can guide nonprofits in determining the most important issues to incorporate into crisis planning. A sound crisis communication plan can build the resilience capacity of a nonprofit organization. Generally, crisis communication plans include the following elements:

- Purpose and overview of the plan
- An explanation of how to use the plan
- Details of the crisis team
- A written crisis communication policy
- A list of potential or foreseeable crisis
- A list of stakeholders
- Prepared messages and materials
- An emergency phone tree (for internal use)
- A detailed crisis communication plan
- A list of communication channels
- A decision tree for actions and considerations
- An after-crisis review plan

Communicating with internal and external stakeholders is a key goal of the crisis communication plan. Nonprofit crises can provide a new way to determine who is most important to the organization. Communication informs stakeholders, influences their perceptions, motivates community action and allows for public perception to be maintained or restored. Nonprofits must identify and understand stakeholder needs and expectations in order to best communicate with them.

Once the crisis communication plan is finalized, it should be implemented. Implementation can include the initiation phase, the instruction phase and the adjustment phase, during which the crisis team introduces the plan and solicits organizational feedback, ensures understanding of the plan and makes any necessary changes. After a crisis occurs, it is important to go back to the plan for evaluation and integrate any additional feedback. Reassessment of the crisis communication plan and the entire organization's planning process highlights how nonprofit organizations can adapt to change and can continue operations.

Crisis is only one current threat to nonprofits. New challenges facing the current workforce include competition, change in political leadership and priorities, technology shifts, communication expectations on various platforms and of course continuing remote work through and beyond the pandemic. To address these challenges before they lead to crisis, nonprofits must lead and plan with a strategic focus, communicate effectively and continue to evaluate operations to ensure the organization is delivering social value. This will require an organizational investment in capacity building.

As nonprofits move from crisis situations, leaders should consider their strategic priorities, with particular focus on better understanding what mission success would look like for the organization, what value the organization is providing, balancing competing voices and priorities and understanding how equity is reflected. Crisis may require leaders to work more hours and shift operations. The most important preparedness work that can be done in nonprofits is to envision what services will need to be provided a week, month and year after a crisis. After any large-scale crisis event, there may be no return to normal; however, there will eventually be a new normal. The services and programs that were offered before a crisis may no longer be needed within the community and the organization may have to turn to new partnerships or opportunities.

Through all crisis situations, nonprofits should remember the importance of compassion. Showing compassion to crisis impact individuals, survivors, stakeholders and the community, particularly through crisis communication, suggests that the nonprofit cares about what is happening in the community and is informed on important issues that are impacting their stakeholders. Often crises involve more than just one organization. Showing solidarity with partners and other community groups suggests the organization supports them and has the best interest of the community in mind. Additionally, nonprofits should always keep in mind that many crises disproportionately impact communities of color and underrepresented groups. In many cases, the individuals served by nonprofits are also the most vulnerable in community disasters. This is often due to a disruption in critical services. Compassion for these groups can help organizations prioritize programming and limiting disruptions for the groups that rely on their services.

This text has presented ample literature on best practices in crisis communication for nonprofits and provided tools for nonprofits to better position themselves for responding to crises by developing an appropriate crisis communication plan. The text is designed for use by nonprofit practitioners and educators; however, several research gaps are uncovered that require empirical attention among communication and nonprofit management and leadership scholars. These include a need for more work in understanding governance structures that work best in crisis response, a renewed attention to handling communication in stacked crisis situations (where the organization is facing multiple crises at once) and how to address equity in crisis planning. These research areas will provide additional insight for practitioners who are crisis planning.

The final chapter of the text presents four distinct case studies nonprofit organizations can utilize to apply what they have learned. These case studies highlight complex and dynamic aspects of nonprofit organizations and crisis management. The crises faced in these organizations are not unlike those faced by others in similar contexts, though each organization has certain dynamics that may make appropriate responses vary for their organization. The case studies include: Give Kids the World Village and COVID-19, Wounded Warrior Project and Reputation Loss, People Inc. and a Data Breach, and Association of Community Organizations for Reform Now Tax Scandal. The case studies are formatted in a way to provide background on the crisis along with discussion questions to allow participants the ability to analyze the case and determine the type of crisis presented, crisis communication planning elements, roles and responsibilities, stakeholders and strategy implementation.

11 Case Studies

Lauren Azevedo and Brittany "Brie" Haupt

Introduction

In preparing nonprofit organizations to engage in crisis communication planning, case studies are included with the purpose of developing critical thinking and decision-making skills (Boyne, 2012; Carey, 2018; Comfort & Wukich, 2013; Corbin, 2018; McCreight, 2009; Silvia, 2012; Waugh & Sadiq, 2011). These skills are critical to crisis response and management and support the nonprofit organization's role of providing vital services to their communities. Research has concluded that case studies are a reflection style exercise that creates a controllable environment to develop and practice crisis response (Boin, Stern, & Sundelius, 2016; Comfort, 2007; Knox & Haupt, 2015, 2020; Van Wart, 2013; Van Wart & Kapucu, 2011).

Scenarios created for this book are based on true events experienced by nonprofit organizations and represent organizational technical crisis, community technical crisis, organizational social crisis and community social crisis. These case studies highlight complex and dynamic aspects of nonprofit organizations and crisis management. The crises faced in these organizations are not unlike those faced by others in similar contexts, though each organization has certain dynamics that may make appropriate responses vary for their organization. There is no single, simple solution or one correct answer when discussing each case. The purpose of these case studies is to stimulate discussions, debates, strategic planning, reflections and theory to practice learning, while enhancing critical thinking skills and applying lessons learned from this book.

Case Study: Give Kids the World Village and COVID-19

Give Kids the World Village (GKTW) is a nonprofit resort that provides vacations away from hospital visits to critically ill children who want to visit central Florida theme parks (Give Kids the World, 2021). GKTW is different from other nonprofits like Make a Wish because they have an 84-acre resort where

DOI: 10.4324/9781003147480-11

wishes are granted, so that the experience includes accommodations, attractions (such as Disney World, SeaWorld and Universal Studios Orlando), venues and other fun activities. GKTW has served over 176,000 families since they opened in 1986 (Elliott, 2021). The mission of GKTW is as follows:

> Give Kids The World Village is an 89-acre, whimsical nonprofit resort in Central Florida that provides critically ill children and their families with magical weeklong wish vacations at no cost. When wish granting organizations from around the world receive a request from a critically ill child who wishes to visit Orlando and its world renowned theme parks, Give Kids The World fulfills all of these wishes – providing every child and his/her family with an all-inclusive experience that includes transportation, accommodations, all meals and snacks, donated theme park tickets, nightly entertainment, daily gifts and more. Since its founding in 1986, Give Kids The World has welcomed more than 177, 000 children and families from all 50 states and 76 countries.

GKTW has a special relationship with the Walt Disney World Resort, as they are a founding partner and important collaborator of the organization. According to the organization, "For many families with children who have a life-threatening illness, taking a trip to Walt Disney World is a dream that is far beyond reach. With Walt Disney World's support, Give Kids The World makes that dream come true at the Village and all four of Walt Disney World's parks" (Give Kids the World, 2021). When staying at the Village, visitors receive Disney paraphernalia and necessary assistance at the parks for families to enjoy the attractions as comfortably as possible. Families also receive access to a designated "Wish Lounge" as a comfortable resting place while at the parks.

GKTW has a 10 member leadership team led by Pamela Landwirth who serves as the President and Chief Executive Officer. Landwirth has been in her position since 1995 and is responsible for Village operations and organizational strategic advancement initiatives. GKTW also has a strong Board of Directors, with representatives from several central Florida businesses and theme parks. GKTW has a media contact listed on their website for media inquiries.

The COVID-19 outbreak in the United States began in January 2020 and quickly became the deadliest disease in U.S. history. The Centers for Disease Control (CDC) and political leaders recommended physical distancing in March 2020 to help curb the spread of the virus. In June 2020, GKTW announced its indefinite closure due to COVID-19 and laid off 171 employees (Santich, 2020). Landwirth announced via social media that "unforeseen circumstances directly related to COVID-19" impacted the closure (Santich, 2020). According to Santich (2020),

An initial statement from the charity — later removed — said the closure followed a decision by the Make-A-Wish Foundation, which helps to cover expenses for many of the 8,000 families who stay at the village each year, not to schedule additional wishes that involve travel or large groups.

Certain health disparities in combination with housing situations, work circumstances and other health factors have put some groups, particularly racial and ethnic minorities and those with compromised health, at higher risk of infection, severe illness and death (CDC, 2021). With this in mind, the organization could not find a way, initially, to safely provide services for critically ill children and their families. During the closure, the organization still requested financial assistance to continue maintenance and landscaping of their grounds and did receive assistance from the federal Paycheck Protection Program.

GKTW took a thoughtful and phased approach to opening their doors, starting with limited families and increasing numbers over time (Elliott, 2021). Experts from a local Children's Hospital worked closely with the organization to develop a COVID-19 safety plan for attendees and staff. Before reopening, GKTW undertook a giving campaign to support other local nonprofits that were impacted by COVID-19, including food donations to the Second Harvest Food Bank, sending "Boxes of Hope" to children whose wishes were postponed due to the pandemic, assisting with Toys for Tots donations during their "Night of a Million Lights" event, with lights donated by Walt Disney World, and letting other organizations use their property during closures (Elliott, 2021).

After ten months, Pamela Landwirth sent an open letter to constituents stating that Give Kids the World Village began a phased reopening in January 2021 with enhanced health and safety guidelines. More than 6,000 children's wishes were delayed during the organization's closure (Give Kids the World, 2021). The COVID-19 protocols and guidelines have been continuously revised and modified throughout the ongoing pandemic, based on "evolving industry standards and methodologies, public health and governmental directives, and advancing scientific knowledge on the transmissibility of COVID-19" (Give Kids the World, 2021). These health and safety guidelines include: mask wearing, physical distancing, cleaning and sanitation, revised work and sick policies, COVID-19 training, in addition to safety enhancements at key operational areas including public spaces, rides and attractions, and employee facilities (Give Kids the World, 2021).

Discussion Questions

1. What type of crisis is presented in this case?

2. Who is (or should be) on the crisis team? Who is the crisis communication coordinator in this example?
3. What was the role of the media in this case?
4. Who are the stakeholders in this situation?
5. How should this organization navigate a decision tree?
6. What communication strategy should be deployed?
7. How can this organization improve their crisis communication plans for a future similar crisis?

Case Study: Wounded Warrior Project and Reputation Loss

The Wounded Warrior Project (WWP) was formed in 2003 by a veteran and friend group in Roanoke, Virginia, as a way to help injured service people. The nonprofit provides programs and services for wounded veterans (Wounded Warrior Project, 2021). The WWP's focus is on wounded veterans who served on or after September 11, 2001, and offers programs related to networking and access to resources, mental wellness, physical wellness, career and veteran benefits, and independence programs. The organization also assists family members and caregivers of Wounded Warriors. The mission of the organization is "to honor and empower Wounded Warriors who incurred a physical or mental injury, illnesses, or wound, co-incident to your military service on or after September 11, 2001" (Wounded Warrior Project, 2021).

The organization seemed to be thriving with a captivating mission and celebrity endorsements up until 2016, when the *New York Times* and the Colombia Broadcasting System (CBS) reported allegations of lavish spending and financial mismanagement. More specifically, CBS claimed high fundraising overhead with only 60% of donations to the WWP going to veterans, while similar organizations like Disabled American Veterans Charitable Service Trust and Fisher House spent 96% and 91%, respectively (Reid & Janish, 2016). The negative media attention dropped public support of WWP by 50% (Seck, 2019).

A CBS and *New York Times* report stated that more than 40 former employees came forward to report spending was "out of control" and money was not appropriately spent on mental health services and follow up services for warriors. Spending on extravagant dinners, hotels and alcohol was mentioned, with increases in spending on "conferences and meetings" from USD 1.7 million in 2010 to USD 26 million by 2014, roughly the same amount they spend on their top program related to combat stress recovery (Phillips, 2016; Reid & Janish, 2016). WWP stated 80% of money is spent on veteran programs; however, Charity Watchdog stated only 54-60% of money goes to actually helping service members (McCambridge, 2017; Reid & Janish, 2016).

Additionally, WWP spent hundreds of thousands of dollars designated for lobbying and public relations campaigns in an effort to "deflect criticism of its spending and to fight legislative efforts to restrict how much non-profits spend on overhead" (Phillips, 2016) as the organization was under increased scrutiny. Within the CBS news report, it was conveyed that WWP declined repeated interview requests from the media source, but offered access to their director of alumni relations and recipient of services (a former veteran), who stated that there was no excessive spending on conferences and lavish resorts and follow-up opportunities were in place for veterans. Many employees who came forward to the media asked to remain anonymous due to fear of retaliation, as the *New York Times* reported, according to Mr. Chick, a former supervisor in WWP, the organization would swiftly fire employees who leaders saw as a "bad cultural fit" (Phillips, 2016). Approximately 18 employees were fired for such claims as poor cultural fit or insubordination (Phillips, 2016), suggesting a lack of concern from WWP over people and a higher concern over profit and results.

Months after these reports went public, WWP's Chief Executive Officer Steve Nardizzi and Chief Operations Officer Al Giordano were fired and donations plummeted in 2017 (Seck, 2019). This came after complaints of leadership's reckless spending at the expense of wounded warrior programming. For instance, the *New York Times* reported a staff meeting in a 5-star Colorado hotel, where Mr. Nardizzi rappelled down into the crowd, costing about USD 1 million (Phillips, 2016).

An investigation by the Better Business Bureau in 2017 helped to clear WWP of its lavish spending, finding in its Wise Giving Alliance Report that spending was in line with its current mission and programs (Wax-Thibodeaux, 2017). By 2018, finances began to recover by approximately 16% (up to USD 246 million), likely thanks to a new CEO who arrived later in 2016. WWP has since cut back on staff outings and high ticket events and changed advertising strategy in an effort to rebuild public trust (Seck, 2019). The Charity Navigator ranking has also slowly increased their rating with marginal improvements through 2018. As of 2022, the Charity Navigator score is 86.49, giving it a 3-star rating (Charity Navigator, 2022).

Discussion Questions

1. What type of crisis is presented?
2. Who is (or should be) on the crisis team? Who is the crisis communication coordinator in this example?
3. What was the role of the media?
4. Who are the stakeholders? How were they impacted?
5. How should this organization navigate a decision tree?
6. What crisis communication strategy should be deployed?
7. How can this organization improve their crisis communication plans for a future similar crisis?

Case Study: People Inc. and a Data Breach

People Inc. is a human service nonprofit organization in New York that provides services for seniors, families and individuals with disabilities to live healthy and productive lives. Their mission is for individuals with disabilities or others with specific needs to have the support needed to participate and succeed (People Inc., 2021). Founded by a group of parents and professionals in 1970, the organization focuses on needs of those with intellectual disabilities. Their programs center around residential care, community outreach, health care, employment assistance and senior recreation, among other programs, for individuals with disabilities, seniors and their families.

People Inc. has since grown to a large health and human services nonprofit expanding its services in New York. The organization has grown to around 4,000 staff members who serve over 5,000 people of varying abilities and ages at around 200 locations (People Inc., 2021). Collaborators of People Inc. have helped to strengthen their mission and ensure financial stability. Some of their collaborators include People Home Health Care Services, which provides short-term home medical care and assistance for daily living. The Elmwood Health Center, established in 1994 thanks to a capital campaign, offers various health care services for individuals with developmental disabilities. People Inc. also partners with Headway of Western New York to provide services to families that are dealing with traumatic brain injury or other cognitive conditions. Other key partners also help to ensure the success of the organization.

In February 2019, an unknown hacker infiltrated an employee's email account exposing sensitive medical and personal information, such as social security numbers, health insurance details, bank account information, government identification and financial data from clients. The compromised email account was accidental and likely due to a weak password that was susceptible to such an attack (Osborne, 2019). Unfortunately, medical organizations and nonprofits are targets for hackers, as they may be more vulnerable to hackers while also holding sensitive information. Nonprofits may be targeted for a number of reasons, but these may include reasons highlighted by Walker (2019) including: volunteers maintaining websites who have limited expertise or training, websites having good domain authority, credibility and readership, and website donations as they can serve as credit card harvesting grounds. Simply put, often nonprofit websites and domains are not as well maintained, have high traffic and hold personal information like credit cards and social security information. People Inc. hired an external cyber forensics group to investigate their case and help gather information to inform the Federal Bureau of Investigation (Osborne, 2019).

Personal information like social security numbers, driving license numbers, health information and other financial data can significantly impact clients. While it may be simple to replace credit cards, identities cannot be replaced and often require much more hassle for constituents who deal with this privacy loss. Dennis Scrader, the director of marketing communications, stated that the organization notified over 1,000 clients whose accounts and personal information were compromised because of the data breach on May 29, 2019, and offered clients whose information was compromised free credit monitoring. Additionally, a toll free call center for clients whose information was compromised was created for questions (The Nonprofit Times, 2019).

The New York State Information Security Breach and Notification Act requires those conducting business or license computer data which includes private information to disclose any data breach to New York residents. Additionally, they must notify the New York Attorney General, the New York Division of State Police and The Department of State's Division of Consumer Protection. The following statement was released on behalf of People Inc.:

> On February 19, 2019, People Inc. discovered that an unknown individual had gained access to an email account belonging to a People Inc. employee. Upon learning this information, People Inc. immediately reset the password required to access the impacted account. People Inc. also engaged an independent forensics firm to determine what happened and whether personal information was accessed or acquired without authorization as a result of this incident. Through this investigation, People Inc. learned that an email account belonging to a second employee may have been impacted as well. That account is no longer operational. On April 11, 2019, as a result of this investigation, People Inc. learned that the two email accounts contained personal information belonging to some current and former clients. This personal information may have included names, addresses, Social Security numbers, financial account information, medical information, health insurance information, and/or driver's license or other government identification numbers.
>
> People Inc. takes the security of all information very seriously. People Inc. has no evidence indicating that any information aside from the information contained within the two employee email accounts was impacted in connection with this incident. In addition, People Inc. has no evidence that any of the information potentially involved in this incident has been misused. People Inc. has reported this matter to the FBI and will cooperate as necessary to hold the perpetrators accountable.

Notification letters were sent to all potentially impacted individuals on May 29, 2019. The letters include information about this incident and about steps that potentially impacted individuals can take to monitor and help protect their personal information. People Inc. has established a toll-free call center to answer questions about the incident and to address related concerns. The call center can be reached at 855-579-3669. In addition, as a precaution, People Inc. is offering complimentary identity protection services through Experian to potentially impacted individuals. To determine if you qualify for this service, you must obtain verification through the call center. If you have been impacted, information on how to enroll for this service will be made available to you.

Discussion Questions

1. What type of crisis is presented?
2. Who is (or should be) on the crisis team? Who is the crisis communication coordinator in this example?
3. What was the role of the media?
4. Who are the stakeholders? How were they impacted?
5. How should this organization navigate a decision tree?
6. What crisis communication strategy should be deployed?
7. How can this organization improve their crisis communication plans for a future similar crisis?

Case Study: Association of Community Organizations for Reform Now Tax Scandal

In 2009 the Association of Community Organizations for Reform Now (known as ACORN), came under scrutiny after a leaked video exposed questionable tax services (Murdock, 2009; Ohlemacher, 2009). ACORN is a community outreach organization that advocates for low and moderate income families. The organization was known for providing free tax advice and voter registration assistance to over 3 million tax filers; however, the controversy caused the Internal Revenue Service (IRS), along with other government agencies, to sever their ties.

Founded by community activist Stephen Rathke and Gary Delgado, ACORN received over 53 million USD in federal funds to aid its cause. Rathke served as ACORN's chief organizer from 1970 to 2008. Rathke and Delgado created a membership model to assist in developing leaders in low-income neighborhoods. According to Brobeck (1997), ACORN established housing corporations to rehabilitate homes, encouraged banks to offer mortgages and home improvement loans in low-income areas and led "living wage" campaigns in several areas. ACORN served well over 350,000 member families in 850 neighborhood chapters in over 100 cities (Brobeck, 1997).

Yet, it took one video to cause a scandal. Conservative activists James O'Keefe and Hannah Giles posed as pimp and prostitute before engaging with multiple locations of ACORN and asking staff for tax advice regarding how to run an illegal business and use underage girls in a sex trade business. The advice given focused on the activists wanting to set up an international prostitution ring and evade the IRS (CNN, 2009). Hidden cameras were used to video the encounters, showing different instances of ACORN employees interacting with O'Keefe and Giles. Several staff members at various offices believed the activists were joking, but played along with the actors. One staff member later sued both Giles and O'Keefe for recording his conversation without permission, a violation of California law, and settled the case outside of court.

These videos received wide coverage in the media and CEO Bertha Lewis called for a comprehensive external investigation and firing of the staff members involved. Various investigations from Proskauer Rose firm, the Congressional Research Service, New York Attorney General, California Attorney General and the U.S. Government Accountability Office into ACORN's operations resulted in several decisions. For one, the House and Senate voted to sever federal funding to ACORN and any of its subsidiaries (CNN, 2009; Dreier & Martin, 2010; Ohlemacher, 2009). In addition, the U.S. Census Bureau severed its ties with the group for the 2010 national headcount, and then New York Gov. David Paterson ordered state agencies to examine contracts with ACORN. The loss of funds led to the closure of 15 of its 30 state chapters by March 2010 soon followed by closures of the remaining chapters (Associated Press, 2010). On November 2, 2010, its U.S. offices filed for Chapter 7 liquidation effectively closing the organization (Memoli, 2010).

ACORN was not new to the impact of scandals as a 2008 voter registration fraud case came against the organization when Republican groups in Florida and several other states claimed ACORN workers were promoting President Barack Obama's candidacy (CNN, 2009). The investigation led to the arrest of 11 individuals suspected of submitting false information on voter registration cards. The Florida investigation was triggered by ACORN officials who noticed irregularities in forms they were receiving.

Discussion Questions

1. What type of crisis is presented?
2. Who is (or should be) on the crisis team? Who is the crisis communication coordinator in this example?

3. What was the role of the media?
4. Who are the stakeholders? How were they impacted?
5. How should this organization navigate a decision tree?
6. What crisis communication strategy should be deployed?
7. How could a crisis communication plan have impacted operations and reputation?

References

Associated Press. (2010). *ACORN closing in wake of scandal.* Retrieved from https://web.archive.org/web/20100325063906/http://www.foxnews.com/story/0,2933,589768,00.html.
Boin, A., Stern, E., & Sundelius, B. (2016). *The politics of crisis management: Public leadership under pressure.* Cambridge, UK: Cambridge University Press.
Boyne, S. M. (2012). Crisis in the classroom: Using simulations to enhance decision-making skills. *Journal of Legal Education, 67*(2), 311–322.
Brobeck, S. (1997). *Encyclopedia of the consumer movement.* Santa Barbara: ABCCLIO Ltd.
Carey, T. J. (2018). The utilization of client-based service-learning in emergency management graduate curricula for the 21st century. *Journal of Homeland Security Education, 7,* 13–28.
Center for Disease Control (CDC). (2021). *COVID-19.* Retrieved from https://www.cdc.gov/coronavirus/2019-ncov/cdcresponse/index.html.
Charity Navigator. (2022). *Wounded warrior project.* Retrieved from https://www.charitynavigator.org/ein/202370934.
CNN. (2009). *ACORN workers caught on tape allegedly advising on prostitution.* Retrieved from https://www.cnn.com/2009/POLITICS/09/10/acorn.prostitution/.
Comfort, L. K. (2007). Crisis management in hindsight: Cognition, communication, coordination, and control. *Public Administration Review, 67,* 189–197.
Comfort, L. K., & Wukich, C. (2013). Developing decision-making skills for uncertain conditions: The challenge of educating effective emergency managers. *Journal of Public Affairs Education, 19*(1), 53–71.
Corbin, T. B. (2018). Teaching disaster management using a multi-phase simulation. *International Journal of Mass Emergencies & Disasters, 36,* 297–312.
Dreier, P., & Martin, C. R. (2010). How ACORN was framed: Political controversy and media agenda setting. *Perspectives on Politics, 8*(3), 761–792.
Elliott, C. (2021). *Give kids the world village for critically ill children reopens following pandemic pivot.* Retrieved from https://www.prnewswire.com/news-releases/give-kids-the-world-village-for-critically-ill-children-reopens-following-pandemic-pivot-301219441.html.
Give Kids the World. (2021). *The magic returns to the village.* Retrieved from https://www.gktw.org/covid19/.
Knox, C. C., & Haupt, B. (2015). Incorporating cultural competency skills in emergency management education. *Disaster Prevention and Management, 24*(5), 619–634.

Knox, C. C., & Haupt, B. (2020). *Cultural competency for emergency and crisis management.* London, UK: Routledge.

McCambridge, R. (2017, May 25). *Senate committee finds past misrepresentation of finances at wounded warrior project.* Retrieved October 20, 2017, from https://nonprofitquarterly.org/2017/05/25/senate-committee-finds-misrepresentation-of-finances-at-wounded-warrior-project/.

McCreight, R. (2009). Educational challenges in homeland security and emergency management. *Journal of Homeland Security and Emergency Management, 6*(1), 1–9.

Memoli, M. (2010). *ACORN filing for Chapter 7 bankruptcy.* Retrieved from https://www.latimes.com/archives/la-xpm-2010-nov-02-la-pn-acorn-bankruptcy-20101103-story.html.

Ohlemacher, S. (2009). *IRS, ACORN sever ties over scandal.* Retrieved from https://www.seattletimes.com/seattle-news/politics/irs-acorn-sever-ties-over-scandal/.

Osborne, C. (2019). *One of New York's largest nonprofits suffers data breach.* Retrieved from https://www.zdnet.com/google-amp/article/one-of-new-yorks-largest-nonprofits-suffers-data-breach/.

People Inc. (2021). *Mission.* Retrieved from https://www.people-inc.org/about/people-inc/index.html.

Phillips, D. (2016). *Wounded Warrior Project spends lavishly on itself, insiders say.* Retrieved from https://www.nytimes.com/2016/01/28/us/wounded-warrior-project-spends-lavishly-on-itself-ex-employees-say.html.

Reid, C., & Janisch, J. (2016). *Wounded Warrior Project accused of wasting donation money.* CBS News Report. Retrieved from https://www.cbsnews.com/news/wounded-warrior-project-accused-of-wasting-donation-money/.

Santich, K. (2020). *Give kids the world closing indefinitely because of coronavirus; 171 employees laid off.* Retrieved from https://www.orlandosentinel.com/coronavirus/os-ne-coronavirus-give-kids-the-world-village-closed-staff-layoffs-20200609-w63qjheqczagdgcmein7vhumay-story.html.

Seck, H. H. (2019). *After public crisis and fall from grace, Wounded Warrior Project quietly regains ground.* Retrieved from https://www.military.com/daily-news/2019/08/09/after-public-crisis-and-fall-grace-wounded-warrior-project-quietly-regains-ground.html.

Silvia, C. (2012). The impact of simulations on higher-level learning. *Journal of Public Affairs Education, 18*(2), 397–422.

The Nonprofit Times. (2019). *Data security incident at nonprofit People, Inc.* Retrieved from:https://www.thenonprofittimes.com/technology/data-security-incident-at-nonprofit-people-inc/.

Van Wart, M. (2013). Lessons from leadership theory and the contemporary challenges of leaders. *Public Administration Review, 73*(4), 553–565.

Van Wart, M., & Kapucu, N. (2011). Crisis management competencies: The case of emergency managers in the USA. *Public Management Review, 13*(4), 489–511.

Walker, J. (2019, May 6). Why hackers target nonprofit websites and how to defend against it. *Give.* https://givewp.com/cybersecurity-nonprofit-hacker-target/.

Waugh, W. L. Jr., & Sadiq, A. A. (2011). Professional education for emergency managers. *Journal of Homeland Security and Emergency Management, 2*(9), 1–9.

Wax-Thibodeaux, E. (2017, February 8). Wounded Warrior Project cleared of "spending lavishly," report finds. *The Washington Post.* https://www .washingtonpost.com/news/checkpoint/wp/2017/02/08/wounded-warrior -project-cleared-of-spending-lavishly-report-finds/.

Wounded Warrior Project. (2021). *Who we are.* Retrieved from https://www.wou ndedwarriorproject.org/mission.

Appendix: Crisis Communication Planning Worksheet

Pre-crisis

Planning committee members
Purpose of the committee
Roles and responsibilities of committee members
Organizational attributes   • Mission   • Vision   • Goals   • Mandates   • Core values/beliefs   • Objectives

Personnel who will utilize this plan
Organizational resources
Internal communication expectations
External communication expectations
Stakeholders and stakeholder analysis
Meeting times, dates and locations

Additional documents attached

- Initial agreement and relevant notes
- Emergency alert internal
- Decision tree matrix
- Phone tree
- Contact information
- Key messages and scripts
- Media releases
- Training and exercise documents
- Affirmation of leadership support
- Safety protocols
- General crisis communication plan
- _____

Crisis Period

Initial steps

- Crisis team alerted
- Phone tree initiated
- Emergency alert internal disseminated
- Spokesperson designated

Crisis type

Spokesperson and official position

Crisis response goals

Best and worst case scenarios
Crisis communication strategies
Organizational resources for response efforts
Communication and notification channels • Internal messaging • Social media • Mass media • _____
Internal communication guidelines
External communication guidelines

Anticipated impacts and circumvention strategies
Implementation policies and procedures
Assessment and accountability measures
Conflict resolution

Post-crisis

After-action report
Review of crisis communication strategies and effectiveness

Internal impact of crisis communication strategies
External impact of crisis communication strategies
Results of assessments and evaluations of crisis communication plan
Results of assessments and evaluations of organizational policies and procedures

Glossary

Accountability The act of being held responsible for actions, choices or behaviors.

Adjusting phase How organizations adjust their crisis communication plan to the type of crisis they are facing.

After-action report A summary of the crisis and its impact to an organization along with assessment and evaluation of implementation protocols.

Agency theory Theory which suggests that both shareholder wealth and organizational performance is maximized when a board of directors monitors the chief executive's tendency to behave with self-interest.

Alignment approach This approach helps clarify where there are gaps, inconsistencies or conflicts among the various elements of an organization's governance, management, operating policies, systems and procedures.

Apologia A formal defense of an opinion, position or action.

Attributional theory The degree to which individuals or a stakeholder will hold an organization responsible for a crisis.

Board capital The human, structural and social capital that individuals bring to the board to facilitate success.

Board power Having strong board members with potential to implement specific actions and influence stakeholders.

Capacity building Any activity that can improve the ability of a nonprofit to achieve its mission and remain sustainable.

Communication The transfer of information through some channel from one party to another.

Communication channels Methods of communication organized by type and number (i.e., radio, brochures, face-to-face, etc.).

Communication messages Consists of the information provided about hazards and the protective measures are characterized via comprehensibility, specificity and number.

Communication sources Entities characterized by their expertise and trustworthiness.

Community crisis A crisis that is threatening the organization externally.

Community social crisis A crisis involving people that is threatening the organization externally.

Community technical crisis A crisis involving technical issues (procedures, systems, structures or society) that is threatening the organization externally.

Contingency approach   An approach to governance which allows for governance configurations to align with its current structure and environment, making room for organizations to reframe current challenges to a more impersonal, structural or sociological view.

Core values/beliefs   The philosophical lens that directs all the actions of an organization.

Crisis   The perception and impact of an unpredictable event that may escalate, fall under stakeholder scrutiny, jeopardize reputation and stakeholder expectations, or interfere with operations and can generate negative outcomes.

Crisis communication center   A location where crisis managers direct all the emergency support functions and gather all essential personnel. This location includes a crisis response kit with essential items, such as written crisis communication plans, notebooks, pencils, pens, computers, necessary chargers, backup generators, emergency services telephone numbers, list of staff and volunteers, emergency contact numbers, support services, and numbers, media contacts, flashlights, weather radio, blankets, first aid kits, bottled water, snacks and other necessities. The headquarters is also a place to have any relevant files organized and have the ability to prepare reports for distribution.

Crisis communication coordinator   The individual on the crisis team responsible for managing organizational communications during crisis either personally and/or delegating organizational crisis communication to specific individuals.

Crisis communication plan   A clear list of steps for a nonprofit organization to follow in case of an unexpected event and usually consists of specific expected results, objectives and milestones; roles and responsibilities of involved organizations and individuals; specific crisis strategies based on crisis types; resource and support requirements and sources; communication feedback process; review and monitoring process; and accountability processes and procedures.

Crisis period   The time period when a crisis has impacted the organization and the ripple effect of the impact is discernible.

Crisis sensemaking   The way in which leaders and other organizational representatives understand crisis situations and process this information when providing organizational responses.

Crisis team   The diverse group responsible for the organization's response to crises.

Cybersecurity   Taking steps to protect critical systems, operations and information from digital attacks from inside or outside of an organization.

Direct approach This approach is utilized when planners review mandates, mission and conduct a SWOC/T analysis to identify strategic issues.

Direct implementation Changes occur immediately without testing or phased implementation. This implementation strategy is best when the situation is technically and politically simple and immediate action is necessary for system survival in a crisis.

Duty of care A nonprofit board member's responsibility to make good judgment on decisions, or one that a prudent person may make under similar circumstances.

Duty of loyalty A nonprofit board member's responsibility to act in good faith for the best interest of the organization.

Duty of obedience A nonprofit board member's responsibility to adhere to the mission, bylaws and policies, as well as standards of appropriate behavior, in their actions.

Effective communication When the receiver of information understands what the sender (messenger) of the information actually intended.

Ethical communication Communication emphasis on the organization's positive values in place before, during and after the crisis. These values range from honesty, transparency and trustworthiness and are the best predictors of positive renewal.

External communication Information sharing outside of an organization.

External stakeholder People who are impacted by the work of the organization, including service recipients, community partners and community members.

Evaluator This individual documents the outcomes of the tabletop exercise – positive and negative. They also provide feedback on recommendations and needs for future planning and training.

Facilitator This individual controls the flow of a tabletop exercise and keeps time. This individual also encourages discussion and focuses on identifying issues and the solutions presented.

Filtering A barrier to effective communication that happens when the messenger distorts or withholds some information in an effort to manage the receiver's reactions.

Focusing events An event that leads to a spotlight on the policies and procedures related to the disaster.

Full-scale exercise This type of exercise is the most in-depth and real experience for participants. The full-scale exercise incorporates representatives from all stakeholders and community partners. This exercise is not just for internal participants but external participants and allows feedback from external entities.

Functional exercise   This type of exercise takes the tabletop into a simulated crisis environment where a scenario is given and the organization must make decisions as if the crisis were occurring. The added stress and urgency of the simulation allows for participants to practice different procedures and plan elements to see what the impact could be.

Gender and cultural differences (in communication)   A barrier to effective communication that happens when social norms and gender differences can influence emotions expressed or interpreted.

Goals   General statements of how to achieve the various strategies that were created to support the mission statement.

Goals approach   This approach is utilized when organizations first establish goals and objectives and identify goals related to those achieving the goals and objectives.

Governance as a leadership model   A model of governance focusing on leadership. This model addresses critical issues facing the organization by sharing leadership between the executive director and the board.

Governance model   A model of governance proposed by John Carver where the focus of governance is on policy and the policymaking process.

Green tape   Organizational legislative, executive and administrative policies and actions that facilitate effective implementation.

Instructing phase   How the organization prepares and supports entities that are involved in the implementation of the crisis communication plan.

Image restoration theory   Introduced by William Benoit, image restoration theory outlines strategies that can be used to restore one's image in an event where reputation has been damaged. Image restoration theory can be applied as an approach for understanding both personal and organizational crisis situations.

Impression management   A conscious or subconscious process in which individuals or organizations attempt to influence the perceptions of others.

Indirect approach   This approach is useful when planners are unsure of the exact need of the organization but acknowledge issues are impacting performance.

Internal stakeholder   People who have a commitment to serving the organization and include the organization's board members, staff members, volunteers and donors.

Internal communication   Information sharing within an organization.

Interpersonal communication   Communication that happens between a small group of people, as few as two, and is more personal. In these instances, feedback happens immediately.

Issues-tension approach This approach focuses on aspects of human resources, innovation and change, maintenance of tradition, and productivity improvements.

Legitimacy The public belief that an organization is fair and acceptable and operating in a legal manner.

Managerial hegemony theory Suggests that the board's power is limited and control is given to the managers of the organization who will make strategic decisions that will fit their objectives.

Mandates Legislative or financial aspects an organization needs to achieve for funding purposes or to meet specified stakeholders' expectations.

Marketing Activities and messages that can motivate stakeholders to take action toward mission fulfillment and social change.

Mass communication Communication that happens between a larger number of people and includes some sort of mass medium. Examples include websites, radio or news networks or social media.

Mass media Technological channels to send messages to a group of people.

Media communications The exchange of information or ideas through any channel of communication, such as the internet, television, radio, newspapers and magazines.

Mission statement The general idea of how the vision will be achieved.

National emergency communications plan A plan generated by the Department of Homeland Security focusing on national emergency communication and providing guidance to practitioners and administrators.

Nonprofit crisis communication Gathering, processing and disseminating information on behalf of the nonprofit organization during a crisis.

Nonverbal communication Communication without words, such as body language, tone and eye contact.

Objectives Specific milestones the organization is attempting to reach and create its definition of success.

Observer This individual is responsible for passively following the tabletop exercise and providing additional feedback that may not be caught by the participants, facilitator or evaluator.

One-way communication Communication that is linear, meaning communication travels from sender to receiver in an effort to advise, influence or control.

Organizational context The environment or atmosphere of the nonprofit, including the size, structure, operations, formality and culture of a nonprofit organization. It is shaped by several factors, including the mission and programming, community, current laws, community expectations and community needs.

Organizational crisis   A crisis that is threatening the organization internally.

Organizational jargon   A barrier to effective communication that happens when there is use of nonprofit terminology or acronyms that some individual receivers outside of the organization may not understand.

Organizational social crisis   A crisis involving people that is threatening the organization internally.

Organizational technical crisis   A crisis involving technical issues (involving procedures, systems, structures or society) that is threatening the organization internally.

Overloading information   A barrier to effective communication that happens when the messenger overwhelms the receiver with details that distract or confuse the receiver.

Participant   These individuals are willing to engage to the fullest of their ability with tabletop exercises with the mindset that the exercise is meant to identify potential issues and solve problems along with highlighting successes of the exercise.

Perception   A barrier to effective communication that happens when the receiver processes information based on one's own experiences or viewpoints and misses the original messenger's intent.

Phone tree   Hierarchical contact list that holds organizational leadership and the crisis team contact information (names, cell phones, home phones, addresses, email, etc.). The list should specify the responsible party for notification.

Poor listening   A barrier to effective communication that happens when the receiver's capacity to listen is insufficient regardless of the messenger's skill in communicating.

Positive renewal   Incorporating optimism into communication and keeping the organization's purpose and mission in mind to support renewal.

Positive rhetoric   Connects to the leadership who would inspire others to stay committed to the cause.

Post-crisis period   The time period when the crisis has reached some level of resolution and operations of the organization are resumed.

Post-crisis review   A review to be completed immediately following a crisis, which includes tying up loose ends with stakeholders, recognizing responders who helped during the crisis, reviewing response actions, ensuring media messages were consistent and updating communication plans and the strategic plan, as necessary.

Pre-crisis period   The state of an organization prior to a crisis occurring.

Rational decision-making theory Developed by Herbert Simon (1979), this theory posits that each individual makes decisions based on logical reasons and facts.

Renewal discourse This discourse incorporates four theoretical objectives that highlight a crisis as an opportunity for organizational learning, ethical communication, prospective vision and positive rhetoric.

Resilience capacity The ability of an organization to manage change or disruptions in such a way that the organization can recover quickly.

Resource dependency theory One way to understand how external resources can impact nonprofit behavior. The theory suggests that organizational survival depends upon its ability to obtain and maintain resources.

Rhetorical analysis Analyzing how effectively an individual or organization communicates their message or argument to their intended audience.

Risk communication A process of sharing information about hazards, risks, vulnerability, assets and adaptive mechanisms within organizations or with the public. The process is intentional and goal directed.

Risk management A process of ascertaining an organization's legal, financial and reputation risks and actively working to avoid them.

Semantics A barrier to effective communication that happens when there are language differences between the sender and receiver, which may also include use of regional or unfamiliar expressions or difficulty understanding accents.

Sharing phase Focuses on how the organization shares information on their crisis communication plan along with any adaptations.

Situational assessment A systematic way to collect information so that planning decisions are informed.

Situational crisis communication theory Developed by Coombs (2012), this theory is a prescriptive approach that evaluates the reputational threat posed by the crisis situation and then recommends crisis response strategies based upon the reputational threat level.

Social capital Social resources including relationships, norms, trust and values.

Staged implementation Implementation will occur in stages or waves.

Stakeholder Anyone with an interest or a "stake" in the organization.

Stakeholder theory Offers implications on management and ethics for constituencies impacted by organizational entities (such as staff or volunteers). The theory suggests that leaders prioritize stakeholders based on their respective power.

Storytelling   Sharing accounts or examples of the nonprofit's work and impact. It is a tool used in communication that can help explain what an organization does and the type of impact it makes.

Systems analysis approach   This approach is the most complicated approach as it focuses on understanding the entire organization as a complex system and intends to understand all the mechanisms within.

Tabletop exercise   This type of exercise incorporates more coordinated discussions among participants to discuss the crisis communication plan and engage the participants in how they would react. A facilitator is helpful in this process and can provide additional information or nuances to the exercises to add more depth and complexity.

Tripartite model of governance   A model of nonprofit governance where the focus of the board is on the organization's mission and engaging in strategic planning to ensure mission congruence with activities. The three integral parts of this governance style include the board, executive director and staff.

Two-way communication   Communication that includes both the message from sender to receiver and feedback from the receiver back to the sender to ensure the message has been received.

Verbal communication   Any written or oral communication using words, such as speeches and conversations.

Vision of success approach   This approach is utilized when an organization develops a "best" picture of the organization in the future and identifies issues that could prevent this from being achieved.

Vision statement   The overarching idea of what the organization is trying to accomplish.

Visual strategy mapping approach   This approach involves creation of word-and-arrow diagrams in which statements about potential actions the organization might take, how they might be taken and why are linked by arrows indicating the cause–effect or influence relationships.

Walkthrough   This type of exercise is useful for very basic training and is focused on familiarizing participants with their roles and responsibilities. It is less time-consuming and can provide a space for everyone to get on the same page.

Index

For Product Safety Concerns and Information please contact our EU
representative GPSR@taylorandfrancis.com
Taylor & Francis Verlag GmbH, Kaufingerstraße 24, 80331 München, Germany

9 7 8 1 0 3 2 4 3 5 3 9 8